Edexcel GCSE

History B

Schools History Project

Medicine and treatment (Option 1A)
and The transformation of surgery
c1845–c1918 (Option 3A)

Cathy Warren   Nigel Bushnell
Series editor: Angela Leonard

A PEARSON COMPANY

Published by Pearson Education Limited, a company incorporated in England and Wales, having its registered office at Edinburgh Gate, Harlow, Essex, CM20 2JE. Registered company number: 872828

www.heinemann.co.uk

Edexcel is a registered trade mark of Edexcel Limited

Text © Pearson Education Limited 2009
First published 2009

13 12 11 10
10 9 8 7 6 5 4 3

British Library Cataloguing in Publication Data
A catalogue record for this book is available from the British Library

ISBN 978 1 84690 440 0

Produced and edited by Florence Production Ltd, Stoodleigh, Devon
Typeset & Illustrated by HL Studios, Long Hanborough, Oxford
Original illustrations © Pearson Education Limited 2009
Cover design by Pearson Education Limited
Picture research by Ginny Stroud-Lewis
Cover photo/illustration © Corbis/Bettmann
Printed in China (CTPS/03)

Websites
There are links to relevant websites in this book. In order to ensure that the links are up to date, that the links work, and that the sites are not inadvertently linked to sites that could be considered offensive, we have made the links available on the Heinemann website at www.heinemann.co.uk/hotlinks. When you access the site, the express code is 4400P.

Disclaimer
This Edexcel publication offers high-quality support for the delivery of Edexcel qualifications.

Edexcel endorsement does not mean that this material is essential to achieve any Edexcel qualification, nor does it mean that this is the only suitable material available to support any Edexcel qualification. No endorsed material will be used verbatim in setting any Edexcel examination/assessment and any resource lists produced by Edexcel shall include this and other appropriate texts.

Copies of official specifications for all Edexcel qualifications may be found on the Edexcel website – www.edexcel.com

Acknowledgements

The author and publisher would like to thank the following individuals and organisations for permission to reproduce material:

Photographs

akg-images pp. 8, 11, 16, 77; Alamy/Inspire Stock Inc. p. 3; Alamy/Janine Wiedel Photolibrary p. 54; Alamy/Lordprice Collection p. 90; Alamy/Mary Evans Picture Library pp. 2, 8, 14; Alamy/Peter Scholey p. 113; Alamy/Phototake Inc. p. 68; Alamy/Picture Partners p. 53; Alamy/Pictures by Rob p. 107; Alamy/Robert Estall Photo Agency p. 71; Alamy/Rodger Tamblyn p. 98; Alamy/Syner-Comm p. 47; Alamy/The London Art Archive pp. 10, 20; Alamy/The Print Collector pp. 3, 10, 92; Alamy/Trinity Mirror/Mirrorpix p. 54; Art Archive/Biblioteca Nazionale Turin/Gianni Dagli Orti p. 16; The Book of Days p. 88; Bradford Museum and Libraries p. 97; Bridgeman Art Library/Bibliotheque de la Faculte de Medecine, Paris, France/Archives Charmet pp. 136–137; Bridgeman Art Library/Bibliotheque Nationale, Paris, France/Archives Charmet p. 3; Bridgeman Art Library/British Library, London, UK p. 76; Bridgeman Art Library/British Library, London, UK/© British Library Board. All Rights Reserved p. 75; Bridgeman Art Library/Private Collection pp. 89, 106; Bridgeman Art Library/The Royal College of Surgeons, London p. 109; City of London p. 100; Corbis/Aristede Economopoulos/Star Ledger p. 135; Corbis/Bettmann pp. 3, 11, 56, 115, 118, 122; Corbis/Heckmann/dpa p. 52; Corbis/Hulton-Deutsch Collection p.122; Corbis/The Art Archive p. 11; Crown Copyright p. 87; Downs Bros Catalogue of Surgical Instruments and Appliances 1900 p. 134; Getty Images/Hulton Archive pp. 100, 101; Getty Images/Popperfoto p. 3; The Gillies Archive of Plastic Surgery p. 133; Imperial War Museum pp. 40, 132; iStockPhoto/Efendi Kocakafa p. 150; iStockPhoto/Chris Schmidt p. 150; iStockPhoto/Alex Slobodkin p. 150; iStockPhoto/Stockphoto4u p. 152; iStockPhoto/ZoneCreative p. 150; Liverpool Record Office/E. Chambré Hardman Archive p. 44; Mary Evans Picture Library pp. 22, 26, 27, 30, 32, 44, 49, 91, 92, 94, 96, 100; Mary Evans Picture Library/Illustrated London News Ltd p. 28; Mary Evans Picture Library/Mary Evans ILN Pictures p. 25; Museum & Archives Service Great Ormond Street Hospital for Children NHS Trust p. 34, 35; NHS pp. 52, 62; PA Photos/Andy Butterton/PA Archive p. 99; Science & Society Picture Library/Science Museum p. 2; Science Photo Library pp. 2, 56, 111, 116, 138, 147; Science Photo Library/A. Barrington Brown p. 56; Science Photo Library/Dr Jeremy Burgess p. 16; Science Photo Library/Mehau Kulyk p. 3; Science Photo Library/Sheila Terry p. 3; Science Photo Library/Simon Fraser/Royal Victoria Hospital, Newcastle-upon-Tyne p. 53; Science Photo Library/Tom McHugh p. 2; Science Photo Library/TEK Images p. 2; Shutterstock/Yuri Arcurs p. 55; Shutterstock/Brasiliao-media p. 121; Shutterstock/Jerome Whittingham pp. 72–73; Unknown p. 11; Wellcome Library, London pp. 2, 3, 12, 13, 26, 28, 31, 33, 62, 68, 73, 79, 106, 107, 108, 110, 113, 117, 119, 121, 126, 127, 132, 135, 140.

Written sources

Source C, p. 109, with thanks to I. Dawson and I. Coulson, *Medicine for Edexcel: An SHP Study in Development*, Hodder Murray, 2001; Source B, p. 114, A.J. Youngson, *The Scientific Revolution in Victorian Medicine*, Holmes & Meier, 1979; Source C, p. 123, K. Haeger, *An Illustrated History of Surgery*, Harold Starke Publishers (History of Surgery), 1988, p. 211; Source A, p. 128, Joseph Lister quoted in J.H. Tiner, *Louis Pasteur – Founder of Modern Medicine*, Mott Media, Milford, Michigan, 1990, p. 111.

Written sources have been freely adapted to make them more accessible for students.

Every effort has been made to contact copyright holders of material reproduced in this book. Any omissions will be rectified in subsequent printings if notice is given to the publishers.

Contents

◼ Option 1A: Medicine and treatment

◼ Medicine and treatment c1350–c1750

◼ Medicine and treatment c1750–c1900

◼ Medicine and treatment c1900 to present day

◼ Extension Study: Medicine and public health from Roman Britain to c1350

Welcome to this Edexcel GCSE History B: Schools History Project Resource

Option 1A: Medicine and treatment and 3A: The transformation of surgery c1845–c1918

These resources have been written to fully support Edexcel's new GCSE History B: Schools History Project redeveloped specification. This specification has a focus on change and development through studies of societies in depth and of key themes over time. Written by experienced examiners and packed with exam tips and activities, the book includes lots of engaging features to enthuse students and provide the range of support needed to make teaching and learning a success for all ability levels.

How to use this book

Edexcel GCSE History B: Schools History Project Medicine and Surgery is divided into the two units that match the specification. Unit 1 begins with the Core Content which all students have to cover, followed by the two Extension Studies, of which students need to answer questions on one. At the end of each section of Core Content (pages 16–17, 36–37 and 56–57) there is a spread devoted to source skills. This has been designed for those studying option 3D The Work of the Historian but will help all students build up source skills and analysis. Unit 3 contains guidance, instruction and practice questions on the source requirements for the exam.

Features of this book

- **Learning outcomes** structure learning at the start of each topic.

- **FASCINATING FACTS** give learning extra depth.

- **Key words** are highlighted and defined for easy reference.

- A topic **Summary** captures the main learning points.

- **Before...** and **After...**
  These give information about what has happened before and after the period studied to help you piece everything together.

- **Activities** provide stimulating tasks for the classroom and homework.

 A dedicated suite of revision resources for complete exam success. We've broken down the six stages of revision to ensure that you are prepared every step of the way.

Zone In! How to get into the perfect 'zone' for your revision.

Planning Zone Tips and advice on how to effectively plan your revision.

Know Zone A checklist of things you should know, revision activities and practice exam questions at the end of each unit and at the end of both Extension Studies in Unit 1.

Don't Panic Zone Last-minute advice for just before the exam.

Exam Zone An overview of what you will have to do in the exam, plus a chance to see what a real exam paper will look like.

Zone Out What do you do after your exam? This section contains information on how to get your results and answers to frequently asked questions on what to do next.

Results**Plus**

These features are based on how students have performed in past exams. They are combined with expert advice and guidance from examiners to show you how to achieve better results.

There are four different types of ResultsPlus features throughout this book:

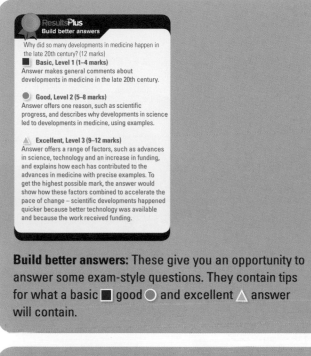

Build better answers: These give you an opportunity to answer some exam-style questions. They contain tips for what a basic ■ good ○ and excellent △ answer will contain.

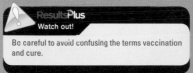

Watch out! These warn you about common mistakes and misconceptions that examiners frequently see students make. Make sure that you don't repeat them!

Maximise your marks: These are featured in the KnowZone. They include an exam-style question with a student answer, examiner comments and an improved answer so that you can see how to build a better response.

Top tip!: These provide examiner advice and guidance to help improve your results.

Medicine and treatment

Introduction

This unit will look at developments in medicine from Roman Britain up to the present day. It is separated into the following sections:

- Medicine and treatment c1350–c1750
- Medicine and treatment c1750–c1900
- Medicine and treatment c1900 to present day
- Medicine and public health from Roman Britain c1350
- Public health from c1350 to present day.

You will be asked to think about what changed, why and why at that particular time; whether the change was an improvement; what didn't change and why it didn't.

These pictures show you some of the topics you will study. The leper is an example of someone suffering from an infectious disease in the Middle Ages – nothing could be done to cure leprosy at the time. We also see how care for the sick has changed over the years: the second picture is of Florence Nightingale treating sick and wounded men during the Crimean War. The third picture shows how science has given us ways to prevent disease and improve people's health – it is a picture of a vaccine for meningitis C.

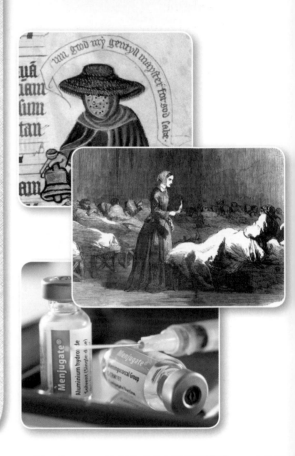

| Before 3000 BCE: Prehistoric | 3000 BCE to 500 BCE: Ancient Egypt | 1000 BCE to 250 BCE: Ancient Greece | 300 BCE to 600 CE: Ancient Rome |

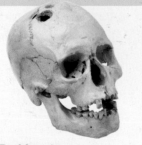

Prehistoric
There is no written evidence, but we have pictures and skeletons that give us some clues about health and medicine.

Ancient Egypt
We have some written evidence and more paintings and artefacts that give us more clues about health and medicine (such as mummies and lists of herbal remedies).

Ancient Greece
By this time we have a wider range of evidence, including pictures, remains of temple buildings and written records from doctors.

Ancient Rome
Now we have even more evidence, such as medical texts, pictures and buildings such as public baths and aqueducts.

Key themes as you work through each period will be:

- What did people think caused illness?
- How did they try to treat and prevent illness?
- Who cared for the sick?
- Was there any progress in medicine?
- What factors affected the developments in medicine?

Activity

1 Look at these pictures of doctors (labelled A to D) and put them in chronological order – that means from the earliest in time to the latest.

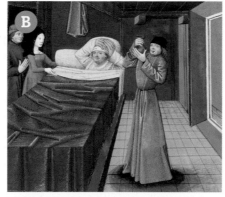

B *A doctor inspecting a patient's urine.*

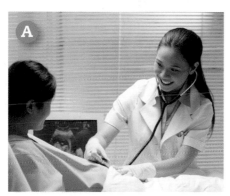

A *A female doctor examining a pregnant woman.*

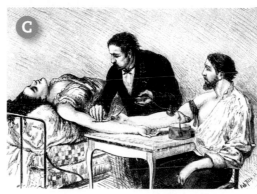

C *A doctor carrying out bloodletting.*

D *A plague doctor, wearing a mask.*

| 400 CE to 1500 CE: Middle Ages | 1500 to 1750: The Medical Renaissance | 1750 to 1900: The Industrial revolution | 1900 to present: The modern period |

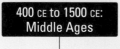

Middle Ages
For this period we can look at evidence from medical texts (both handwritten manuscripts and the earliest printed materials) and buildings such as hospitals.

The Medical Renaissance
This was a period when printed texts became more widely available, so we have a much wider range of evidence.

The Industrial revolution
For this period we have a wide range of evidence, such as public records, photographs and medical instruments.

The modern period
For this period, as well as a wide range of written evidence, buildings and instruments, we can also use oral accounts and film.

Answer to Activity 1: the correct order is B, D, C, A.

1.1 Medicine and treatment c1350–c1750: introduction

This section begins with examining medicine and treatment in 1350 before moving on to discover what changed and what remained the same in the period up to 1750. The key words on this page are important throughout this section so you may need to refer back to this page until you understand what they mean!

Before...

- The Ancient Greeks developed an explanation for ill health based on natural causes rather than supernatural ones.
- The Romans introduced good standards of public health throughout their empire.
- When the Romans left Britain in the 5th century, much of their civilisation gradually collapsed as England was then invaded by the Angles, Saxons, Vikings and then Normans.

After...

- Not until the late 18th and 19th centuries were there significant advances in the understanding of the causes of ill health and a greater use of science and technology in medicine.

ResultsPlus
Watch out!

Many students assume that life in the Middle Ages was the same for everyone. Remember that there was great variation between different areas of the country and different groups within society.

FASCINATING FACT
The fur worn by rich people kept them warm but also tended to attract fleas.

Apothecary: A person who made medicines and ointments using ingredients such as herbs and spices

Black Death: A highly infectious disease that spread throughout Europe in the mid-14th century

Bloodletting: The drawing of blood from a patient by a doctor

The Church: The international organisation of all Christian believers

Four Humours: A theory that developed in Ancient Greece to explain illness

Medieval: A name for the 'Middle Ages', the period between the Ancient World (which ended when the Romans left Britain) and the Renaissance of the 16th and 17th centuries

Physician: A trained doctor

Reformation: A period of challenges and divisions within the Christian Church

Renaissance: A period in the 16th and 17th centuries when people thought they were reviving Ancient Greek and Ancient Roman culture but also made new discoveries

Royal Society: A group set up in 1660 to enable educated people to discuss scientific ideas

Supernatural: Forces outside normal nature that some people believe can affect events, for example, God, charms and luck, witchcraft or astrology

1348
Black Death reached Britain

1543
Vesalius published *The Fabric of the Human Body*

1628
Harvey published *On the Motion of the Heart and Blood in Animals*

1660
Royal Society established

1665
Plague in London

1.2 What were your chances of a long life if you were born in 1350?

Learning outcome

By the end of this topic you should be able to:

- understand why many people's life expectancy was so low during the Middle Ages

Life expectancy

Nowadays the average life expectancy is around 80 years. In the 1350s it was around 30 years, although the rich, who didn't do manual work and had better diets, might have lived longer. Of course, some individuals lived to be 50, 60 and even 80, but this was unusual.

So what were your chances of a long life? Infant mortality was high. Out of every five children born, there was a high chance that one would die before their first birthday and another would die in childhood. They died from illness, injury, poor living conditions or malnutrition. The remaining three children might grow up and get married and have their own families. Even so, many women died in childbirth and both men and women could die from injuries, while diseases such as smallpox, leprosy and various fevers – called 'agues' – killed people of all ages.

Medicine in the **medieval** period was focused on dealing with infectious diseases but also on treating daily aches and pains. Conditions that we can now treat successfully, such as heart problems, types of cancer or the need for a hip replacement, were less of a problem because fewer people lived to old age. But when these conditions did develop, there was usually no successful treatment for them.

Source A: A medieval home in 1350. Most people only had one room in their home and during the winter they often brought their animals, such as cows and pigs, indoors.

Activities

1 What clues can you see in the above picture of a peasant's home to suggest reasons why people might become ill?

2 Summarise the reasons why life expectancy in medieval times was so much shorter than it is nowadays, using the following headings: Living conditions; Disease; Other reasons.

3 Explain which of these reasons for a short life expectancy would apply to everyone, and which reasons would apply mainly to the poor.

Challenge

4 How far do you think it is still true that richer people in Britain tend to live longer than poorer people? You should be able to think of points to both support and challenge this idea, and make sure you explain why you find some points are stronger than others.

Summary

Average life expectancy was around 30 years due to illness, injury, poor living conditions and malnutrition.

1.3 How far did medical ideas from the Ancient World continue to be used in the Middle Ages?

Learning outcomes

By the end of this topic you should be able to:

● understand that medicine from 1350 to 1750 was still based on ideas from the Ancient World

● understand the idea of ill health being the result of an imbalance in the Four Humours

● provide examples of treatments based on the Four Humours

● explain the link between ideas and treatments and provide examples

The Four Humours

The Ancient Greeks identified four different liquids, or humours, in the body:

● blood
● phlegm (the watery liquid when you sneeze or cough)
● yellow bile (when you are sick)
● black bile (we think this was probably blood in your vomit, which makes the liquid look black).

The Greeks thought that every person had their own individual mix of these **Four Humours** and that if this mix was unbalanced you became ill (see the diagram on this page). So, if you had a temperature, your skin went red and hot because you had too much blood, whereas a dark lump was the result of too much black bile.

They also thought that these humours were linked to the four seasons and their idea of four elements (earth, air, fire and water). Therefore, in winter, which is linked to water, they believed that your body produces too much phlegm and you have to sneeze and cough to get rid of it.

This theory helped to explain why people became ill and sometimes treatment tried to restore the

balance of the Four Humours, for example, by letting out excess blood. However, Hippocrates, the leading Greek doctor, suggested that most treatment should be based on rest, changes in diet and leaving the body to heal itself.

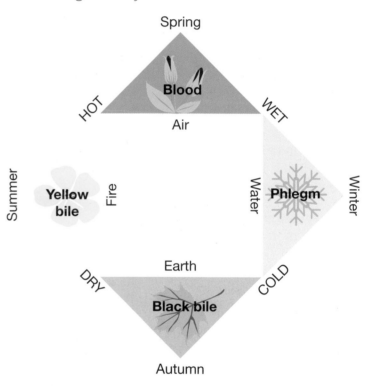

Humour	Season	Element	Qualities	Ancient name
Blood	Spring	Air	Warm & moist	Sanguine
Yellow bile	Summer	Fire	Warm & dry	Choleric
Black bile	Autumn	Earth	Cold & dry	Melancholic
Phlegm	Winter	Water	Cold & moist	Phlegmatic

Galen and the Theory of Opposites

Later, Galen, a doctor working in Rome in the 2nd century CE, developed the Theory of the Four Humours further. He believed very strongly in **bloodletting** as a treatment for almost all illnesses and also suggested that the balance of a person's Four Humours could be restored by his Theory of Opposites. He suggested that, if you had too much phlegm, which is linked to water and cold, you should eat hot peppers; if you had a temperature, you should eat cucumber, which would cool you down.

Galen produced over 350 texts about medicine and surgery, which summarised medical knowledge at the time. He explained his new ideas and linked them with existing theories, making them into one coherent system. He was very confident and boldly claimed that he had now perfected Ancient Greek ideas, and therefore many people believed that there was no point in any further medical research.

Galen in the Middle Ages

Galen's ideas continued to be the basis of medical training throughout the Middle Ages. When the first European medical school was established at Salerno in the 10th century, teaching was based on his ideas and texts rather than students having any practical experience. Treatment was also usually based on Galen's ideas of bloodletting, purging and his Theory of Opposites. However, **physicians** also prescribed medicines based on a wide range of ingredients, such as plants, herbs and spices, and also ground minerals or the bezoar (a stone found in the stomach of goats in Persia).

As learning increased during the 12th century, there was a great deal of interest in the stars and in astrology. Scholars linked these star signs to the Greek idea of the four elements: earth, air, fire and water. These astrological ideas were then linked to Galen's ideas on medicine. For example, doctors believed that an operation on the head should be avoided when the moon is in the sign of Aries.

Physicians often used a handbook, called 'vade mecum', which is Latin for 'Go with me' These manuals would include urine charts where the physician could compare the colour of the patient's urine with the chart to help him diagnose the illness, or a zodiac chart helping the physician to know when to avoid certain treatments. There were also books such as the *Compendium of Medicine* written by Gilbertus Anglicus (Gilbert the Englishman). This was in Latin because it was

intended for educated physicians and helped the physician to diagnose and treat a range of illnesses. Herbals, which described plants and their uses in medicine, were in English because they were used by ordinary people in folk remedies.

Activities

1 Draw an ideas map to show the importance of Galen's work in the Roman period.
2 How far was medicine in the medieval period still based on Galen's ideas?
3 'The continued use of Galen's idea 1000 years after his death shows a lack of progress in medicine.' How far do you agree with this statement?

Summary

Galen's ideas and the Theory of the Four Humours from Roman times continued to be very important in the Middle Ages.

1.4 Medical ideas and practices at the time of the Black Death

Learning outcomes

By the end of this topic you should be able to:

- understand the range of ideas about causes of the Black Death and the various approaches to its treatment
- understand why people turned to religion as an explanation for the Black Death
- explain why people became flagellants
- understand why people continued to use remedies that did not work

The Black Death

People in medieval times lived in small villages and did not travel far, so epidemics of diseases didn't usually spread over the whole country. However, in 1348 a disease reached England that had already killed thousands of people in Europe. About one-third of the population died in an outbreak of bubonic plague that became known as the **Black Death**.

> The bubonic plague was carried by the fleas that lived on black rats; if a flea bit a human, the disease entered the human's bloodstream. As the body tried to fight the illness, the lymph glands swelled into 'buboes'. Of those people who caught the bubonic plague, two out of every three died.

Why were religion and medicine so closely linked?

In Europe in the Middle Ages there were some Jews and Muslims, but most people were Christians and followed the teachings of the Catholic Church.

Source A: This Danse Macabre picture shows the understanding that Death could take anyone, at any time.

Religion was a very important part of people's lives because it provided explanations for so much that happened – bad harvests, the death of an animal, or someone suddenly becoming ill. Religion told them that these things occurred because God was displeased with them, or because God was testing them to see if they stayed faithful even when bad things happened.

The idea that the plague was a punishment or a test from God meant that groups called 'flagellants' walked in procession to the church, whipping themselves, to show God how sorry they were and to ask for his mercy.

Source B: Why did people whip themselves because of the plague?

Other ideas about the plague

Other ideas about the cause of the plague included:

- an unusual positioning of the planets Mars, Jupiter and Saturn (events among the stars and planets were thought to affect events on earth)
- poisonous fumes from volcanoes and earthquakes
- bad air (miasma) from decaying refuse, spread through movements in the air
- an imbalance in the Four Humours
- the activities of groups of outsiders, such as strangers or witches (in Europe they also blamed Jews, but the Jews had been forced to leave England the century before this).

Treatments

Some of the actions people tried were:

- holding a piece of bread against the buboes and then burying it in the ground
- fasting and praying
- eating cool things
- carrying herbs and spices to smell
- walking in procession to a church, saying prayers and whipping each other
- cutting open the buboes and draining the pus
- tidying the rubbish from the streets
- lighting a fire in the room
- keeping the air moving by ringing bells or keeping birds flying around the room
- not letting people enter the town or village from other places or leaving the area themselves.

Because people in medieval times did not know the true causes of the plague, their treatments and remedies were unlikely to be successful, but some people made a lot of money selling fake potions and remedies!

Others decided to eat, drink and enjoy whatever life they had left.

FASCINATING FACT
The idea that a strong smell could overcome the plague led some people to smell the contents of their toilets every morning.

Activities

1 Explain why, in 1348, someone who caught the plague might go to a priest rather than to a doctor.

2 Why did the plague spread more rapidly in towns than in the countryside?

3 Classify people's ideas about the cause of the plague into:

 a) theories based on belief in the supernatural, such as religion, astrology or witchcraft

 b) ideas based on natural causes, such as unbalanced humours or poisonous gases.

4 Divide the list of treatments on this page into:

 a) those aimed at curing the plague

 b) those aimed at preventing the plague.

5 Look at the lists in your answer to question 4; explain which actions you think might have been effective and why.

Challenge

6 Why did people continue to follow the advice of priests and doctors even when so many priests and doctors themselves caught the plague and died?

Role-play

7 A village meeting: one of your villagers has come back from another village with news of many people falling ill and dying. What does he tell the people in the village? What is the response of the villagers? Include ideas from the village priest and a doctor.

Go further

8 Find out about the pneumonic and septicaemic plagues – their causes, symptoms and death rates.

Summary

There was a range of ideas about the cause of the Black Death. Since these were inaccurate, ideas about its treatment and prevention usually had no effect at all.

1.5 Who was responsible for treating the sick in the Middle Ages?

Learning outcome

By the end of this topic you should be able to:

- understand the range of treatments available during the Middle Ages

---

FASCINATING FACT

Some treatments of this period would have worked: for example, honey has natural antiseptic properties, so smearing it on to a sore or wound would have been effective. But hanging a magpie's beak around your neck would probably not have cured your toothache!

Galen's ideas and medical teaching

Medical schools were set up at universities during the 12th century, and books such as those by the English doctor John of Gaddesden (c1280–1361) included knowledge from both Muslim and Christian doctors. However, most physicians' training was based on Galen's ideas. Even though a few human dissections were carried out, they were to demonstrate Galen's teaching while his book was read out loud by the lecturer. Nobody was expected to check whether Galen was right or not.

Galen had lived before Christianity became a major religion, but he believed in a soul and he said that the parts of the body had been created to work together. These ideas fitted well with Christian beliefs and meant that the Church approved of his teachings. Since the majority of education and medical training was controlled by **the Church** and most collections of books were in monasteries, it was very difficult to challenge Galen's ideas.

Who will you go to?

This poor person is feeling very ill. What choices does she have for treatment?

The trained physician

- has had training at medical school and passed exams
- will diagnose you using your urine and astrological information
- administers treatment based on Galen: likely to be bloodletting, purging to balance your humours or herbal medicine
- consults astrology to determine the best approach to treatment
- can be expensive – you pay for each visit, but he has medical knowledge and believes his treatment to be superior to that of **apothecaries** and barber-surgeons
- doesn't mix medicines – you get them from the apothecary
- might not let blood himself – will direct you to the barber-surgeon
- will be male – women physicians were incredibly rare in this period.

The apothecary

- is trained but has no medical qualifications
- mixes various ingredients to produce medicines or ointments for the physician
- may also make you up their own mixture for a price
- is cheaper than having to consult a physician and then pay an apothecary for the same medicine anyway
- is probably male.

ResultsPlus

Watch out!

Students sometimes assume that people in the Middle Ages were stupid because they used supernatural ideas in their medicine.

Students often do not understand that people might try different types of remedies at the same time.

The barber-surgeon

- practises lots of bloodletting; can also pull out rotten teeth and lance boils
  - can even have a go at some basic surgery, such as cutting out bladder stones or amputating limbs
  - uses no anaesthetics, and has a very low success rate for surgery
  - is not trained and is not respected by trained physicians
- can also cut your hair.

Hospital

- was nothing like a modern hospital; was usually for the old or for specific illnesses, such as leprosy – sick people were looked after at home
- was run by monks and nuns: Christianity values caring for others
- after the Reformation in the 16th century some free hospitals were set up in towns, funded by charity.

Housewife-physician

- knew traditional remedies for things such as sore throats, stomach aches or a temperature
- would also be able to deal with broken bones and with childbirth – may have had a reputation as a local 'wise woman'
- used some remedies based on herbs and other plants, and others based on charms and spells
- could be the lady of the manor, who would treat her servants or families living on manor land.

Prayer and pilgrimage

- Many people would also go on pilgrimage to a holy shrine in the hope that they could be cured of an illness.

Women and medicine

There were a few female physicians, such as Trotula, who taught at Salerno medical school in the early 12th century. However, women were not allowed to attend universities, which drove them out of the medical profession by the 14th century. Women continued to work as midwives, but they were expected to have a licence from their bishop to show that they were of good character and would not encourage illegal abortions.

Treatments

Treatment continued to be a mixture of tried and tested herbal remedies, bleeding and purging, and **supernatural** ideas. Trained physicians based their diagnosis and treatment on the Four Humours, often using astrology to decide when to bleed a patient. Healers and patients also showed a belief in the supernatural, so cures might include saying a prayer or holding a lucky charm while the patient was bled to balance their humours. Superstitious cures might include ingredients such as powdered unicorn horn, saying a charm as you drank a medicine or using plants that had to be picked at full moon.

Activities

1 Imagine you are a newly qualified physician who wants to set up business in your local town. Produce an advertisement explaining how knowledgeable you are and what services you offer.

2 Explain why the housewife-physician was less respected than the physician, even though she treated more people.

3 Draw an ideas map to explain how religion was linked to medicine at this time. Use the headings: Ideas about the causes of ill health; Treatment and prevention of ill health; Care for the sick; Medical training.

4 Why did people continue to use remedies that didn't work?

5 Use the information on this page to create a series of 'Top trumps' cards for each of the different people who cared for the sick. Give each person a rating out of five for (a) their knowledge; (b) their experience; (c) the cost of their treatment; and (d) likely success rate.

Summary

There were many different choices of health treatment for the rich, but very few for the poor.

1.6 The impact of the Medical Renaissance (c1500–c1750)

> ## Learning outcomes
>
> By the end of this topic you should be able to:
>
> - understand how far existing ideas were challenged by new discoveries
> - understand the influence of Vesalius
> - understand why Harvey's work had limited impact on medical treatment

Renaissance and Reformation

- **Renaissance** is 'shorthand' for a period in European history when Ancient Greek and Roman ideas became fashionable, among the rich and educated.
- European exploration in Africa and the Americas led to new attitudes and a search for knowledge. Meanwhile changes in religion known as the **Reformation**, led to a decline in the Church's authority, even though most people remained very strongly religious.
- In Britain the **Royal Society** was set up in 1660 by educated people who wished to discuss new ideas.

Vesalius and new ideas about the body

In 1543, Andreas Vesalius, the Professor of Surgery at Padua University in Italy, published an important book called *The Fabric of the Human Body*. This included drawings showing the muscles, nerves, organs and skeleton of the human body based on dissections of corpses.

Vesalius' book had two major impacts. First, even if physicians did not do dissections themselves, they could still learn a great deal about human anatomy from his illustrations. Second, Vesalius discovered that some of Galen's teachings were wrong.

Some examples of Vesalius' corrections

- Galen had said that the heart was divided by a septum that had holes in it to allow the blood to pass through, but Vesalius showed the septum did not have holes in it.
- Galen had said the liver had five parts or lobes, but Vesalius showed the liver did not have any lobes.
- Galen had said the lower jaw was made up of two bones but Vesalius showed that, although this was true in monkeys and pigs, in humans it was a single bone.
- Galen said the sternum had seven parts but Vesalius showed it only had three.

Source A: An illustration from Vesalius' book showing the muscles of the human body.

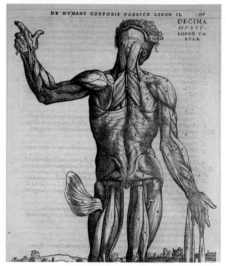

Why was printing important?

The invention of the printing press in Germany in the mid-15th century meant that printed copies of works such as those by Vesalius and which described plants and herbs used in medicine could be produced quickly and cheaply.

Harvey's discoveries

William Harvey, an Englishman, proved even more of Galen's ideas to be incorrect. He worked out through experiment and observation that:

- Veins only carry blood, rather than a mixture of blood and air.
- Blood is not constantly manufactured by the liver and is not used up as it moves around the body (as Galen had taught), but is actually circulated repeatedly around the body.

Harvey published a book in 1628 called *An Anatomical Account of the Motion of the Heart and Blood in Animals*, describing his experiments and explaining how the heart works as a pump circulating blood around the body. He also suggested that the blood must go through tiny blood vessels in order to move from arteries to veins – he was right, but microscopes were not powerful enough to prove that these capillaries existed until much later.

The impact of Renaissance discoveries

There were a number of technological developments, such as mechanisms in pumps and clocks, that helped people to accept the idea of the body functioning as a machine. When the Dutch scientist Antonie van Leeuwenhoek developed better lenses for a microscope, he discovered bacteria, which he described as 'animalcules', in a letter to the Royal Society in 1673.

Nevertheless, it took over 40 years before Harvey's ideas were accepted by other doctors and taught at medical schools. This is because people are often reluctant to accept new ideas if it means accepting that their 'knowledge' is actually wrong, especially as doctors' training was still based on Galen's ideas and physicians did not carry out dissections. Furthermore, Harvey's work was on physiology (how the body's organs function) rather than on the cause or treatment of illness, and so his work did not seem particularly relevant to the work of physicians and the problems of disease.

FASCINATING FACT

Harvey carried out post-mortems on his father and his sister.

Source B: An illustration from Harvey's book, showing an experiment that proved blood flowed only in one direction in the veins, towards the heart.

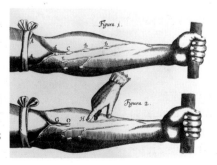

Activities

1 How did Vesalius' work affect medical training?
2 Explain why the invention of the printing press at this time was so important for the work of Vesalius and Harvey.
3 Produce a newspaper front page reporting on Harvey's ideas. Make sure you include quotes by other doctors.

Challenge

4 Prepare a series of true/false statements about medicine in the medieval and Renaissance periods that can be done as a revision quiz or as a starter activity for the next few lessons.

ResultsPlus
Build better answers

Question: Why did the discoveries of the Renaissance have such limited impact on the understanding and treatment of illness? (12 marks)

■ **Basic, Level 1 (1–3 marks)**
Answer gives very general terms and does not provide any examples of Renaissance discoveries.

● **Good, Level 2 (4–9 marks)**
Answer provides excellent descriptions of the Renaissance discoveries of Vesalius, Harvey and the printing press, but does not link directly to the question.

▲ **Excellent, Level 3 (10–12 marks)**
Answer explains why the work of Vesalius and Harvey and the invention of the printing press improved knowledge of anatomy and physiology, but did not improve understanding of disease.

Summary

The Medical Renaissance saw many old ideas about anatomy and physiology challenged, and the printing press spread these ideas faster and more cheaply than before. But there was resistance to change, and there were not many new developments in the understanding of disease itself.

1.7 Change and continuity: how much did medicine change between 1350 and 1750?

Learning outcomes

By the end of this topic you should be able to:

- prepare examination-style answers
- identify examples of both change and continuity within this period
- understand that there were elements of change and continuity in medicine simultaneously throughout this period
- analyse the role of various factors in developments during this period

Source A: A physician telling an apothecary which ingredients to include in a medicine.

Renaissance developments

There were significant changes in people's knowledge and understanding of the human body during the Renaissance period, but very little improvement in the understanding and treatment of illness. When there was a plague epidemic in London in 1665, the treatments used were similar to those used in 1348. Ordinary medical treatment continued to be based on the Four Humours. People also believed that a king's touch could cure them of tuberculosis (TB). Charles II (1630–1685) touched over 8,000 sufferers of the disease in one year. Here are some events and factors affecting the development of medicine during this period:

The Church controlled education and medical training.

The Church discouraged dissection.

Herbal remedies were passed down from one generation to the next.

The microscope was invented

Universities and medical schools were founded in the 12th century.

Some herbal remedies worked.

New plants were discovered when new lands were explored.

The works of Galen were used as the basis for all medical training.

The authority of the Catholic Church decreased.

Many people were reluctant to change the way they did things.

The mechanical pump was invented.

Many people believed that their lives were affected by supernatural events.

The printing press was invented.

Some people felt better after being bled or purged.

Few people could afford to go to a trained physician.

Most minor illnesses and injuries were treated by the women in the family.

Activities

1 Study the list of events and factors affecting developments in medicine on the opposite page. Classify them into two groups:

   a) points leading to progress

   b) points holding back developments so that old ideas continued.

2 Do you think that the period from 1350 to 1750 was a period in medicine of mainly change or mainly continuity (continuing old methods)? Explain your answer.

3 How would your answer to question 2 have been different if the question was about the time period 1350–1500 or 1500–1700? Explain your answer.

4 Go back to the two lists you made in your answer to question 1. Colour code your list to show:

   • the role of religion and beliefs
   • scientific knowledge
   • technological equipment
   • social attitudes.

5 Which of these four factors do you think has been most important in leading to change?

6 Which factor do you think has been most important in maintaining continuity?

7 Draw a Venn diagram like the one below, showing aspects of medieval medicine, Renaissance medicine and aspects that appear in both periods.

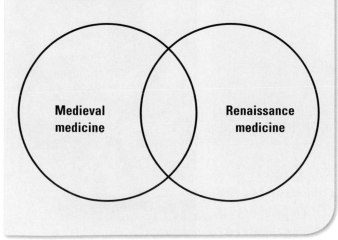

Medieval medicine

Renaissance medicine

ResultsPlus
Build better answers

Question: Why did the discoveries of the Renaissance make little practical difference to medical treatment in the period c1500–c1700? (12 marks)

■ **Basic, Level 1 (1–4 marks)**

Answer offers valid comment but without supporting detail, for example, the discoveries were mainly about anatomy and how the body works.

OR

Answer offers valid details, for example, Vesalius' book *The Fabric of the Human Body* was published in 1543.

● **Good, Level 2 (5–8 marks)**

Answer provides relevant details, for example, describes the Renaissance discoveries of Vesalius and Harvey, or explains the importance of inventions such as the printing press or microscope.

OR

Answer explains how medical training continued to be based on the teachings of Galen.

▲ **Excellent, Level 3 (9–12 marks)**

Answer shows that Renaissance discoveries by Vesalius and Harvey were about anatomy and physiology and that this had little relevance to the understanding and treatment of disease. Answer also shows that medical training did not change and therefore treatment continued to be based on the ideas of Galen and that this was not effectively challenged by a better understanding of the body.

Summary

There were some important changes in knowledge of the body during this period but there was also a great deal of continuity, especially in the ideas about illness and the medical treatments that were used.

1.8 The work of the historian: how much evidence do we have about the role of women in the period 1350–1750?

Learning outcomes

By the end of this topic you should be able to:

- understand the role of women in medicine in the period 1350–1750
- understand the problems historians face when researching a subject where evidence is limited

Researching the role of women

The role of women in medieval medicine is a difficult topic to research because our evidence is so limited. Most people in the period 1350–1750 could not read and write, and although boys might receive an education to become lawyers or merchants, the education for girls (even in wealthy families) was based around running a home. This means that we have very few sources produced by women to tell us about their lives in the medieval period.

Furthermore, the accounts written by men tended to focus on events such as new laws, wars and the actions of the rich. They did not feel that accounts of daily life were important, and we therefore have only a limited amount of sources to tell us about family life and women's activities.

Source A: What do these pictures suggest about the role of women in medieval medicine?

Many women made their own herbal remedies.

Women were usually responsible for the health of the family.

A midwife and female attendant helping a woman through childbirth.

Sometimes we can gather together information from different sources and try to build up a picture of women during the medieval period, but we do not know whether the women in these sources are examples of typical behaviour or unusual cases.

Source B: The legal records of a court case in Paris in 1322.

> Jacoba visited the sick folk, examining their urine, touching, feeling and holding their pulses, body and limbs. After this examination she would say to the sick folk 'I will cure you by God's will, if you will trust in me', making a compact with them and receiving money from them.

This legal record describes how the city's university accused a woman called Jacoba of working without the proper qualifications. A number of people gave evidence that her treatments had been successful and it was suggested that the only reason Jacoba was prosecuted was because she was so successful that male doctors were losing business.

Source C: The Paston family wrote many letters to each other in the 14th century and these include comments about daily illnesses and injuries. Here is an extract from a letter from Margaret Paston. (Treacle or syrup was expected to remove infections.)

> I ask you heartily that you will quickly send me a pot of treacle for I have used that which I had. One of the tallest young men in this parish lies sick and has a great fever. I have sent my Uncle Berney the pot of treacle that you bought for him.

Source D: Lady Grace Mildmay was from a wealthy English family in the 16th century and there are a number of recipes for herbal medicines listed in her papers. Here she is writing about headaches.

> If it arises from phlegm, the face will be full and pale, and the eyes swollen and dark.
> For remedy of the headache, of what kind soever it be, according to the signs of the offending humour, apply cordials or coolers inward and outward.
> If giddiness or other grief in the head have been occasioned by keeping corrupt fluids within the body, then must opening things be given.

Source E: In a book he wrote in 1651, Dr James Primrose complained about women going beyond their proper responsibilities and doing the work of a physician.

> They know how to make a bed well, boyle pottage, and they know many remedies for diseases. But [dealing with ulcers and wounds] can only be known by a skilful physician and women ought not to meddle with them. They take their remedies out of English books but Galen teaches that remedies should be altered according to the person, place, part affected and other circumstances and seeing that these things cannot be attained without much labour and study, I cannot be brought to believe women are able to understand, or perform what they promise.

Source F: Here is an extract from a letter from John Paston to his wife, Margery.

> Send as quickly as possible a large plaster (poultice) for the king's attorney for an ache in his knees. When you send me the plaster you must write to me telling me how long it should stay on the knee. And whether he must wrap any cloth around the plaster to keep it warm.

Activities

1. How much can the historian generalise about the role of women in medicine in the period c1350–c1750 from individual examples (such as the three women – Jacoba, Margaret Paston and Lady Grace Mildmay – named in the sources in this section).

2. How much weight should the historian put on the complaints of Dr Primrose in Source E?

3. Is it reasonable for historians to generalise about the situation of women when we have only a few pieces of surviving evidence spread over a long period of time? Explain your answer.

4. How do you think the historian can deal with the problems caused by the lack of sources about medieval women?

2.1 Medicine and treatment c1750–c1900: introduction

This section begins with examining the situation in 1750 before moving on to discover what changed and what remained the same in the period up to 1900. The key words on this page are important throughout this section so you may need to refer back to this page until you understand what they mean!

Before...

In the medieval and Renaissance periods, people did not know what caused diseases to spread, and medical treatment was based on theories such as the Four Humours or miasma (bad air). During the Reformation in the 16th century, the influence of the Church on medical training and treatment began to decline, while a better understanding of the body began to develop, based on a more scientific approach to knowledge and understanding.

After...

In the modern period, the role of science and technology improved our ability to diagnose and treat illness, but there was also an emphasis on prevention of illness through **vaccinations**, genetic research and changes in lifestyle. Women have become far more involved in professional medicine, and the government has taken on a wide range of responsibilities within public health.

Anatomy: The structure of the body, for example, bones, nerves, muscles

Epidemic: A severe outbreak of an infectious disease

Industrial: Connected to industry and manufacturing

Industrial revolution: The period c1750–1900 when there were rapid changes in the way work and industry was organised

Inoculation: A way of giving a patient a mild dose of an illness so that the body builds up its immunity

Miasma: The theory that disease is caused by poisonous vapours in the air

Patent medicine: A mixture that has been created by one person or company and is sold under a particular brand name

Pharmacy: A business selling medical drugs; a chemist's

Pharmaceutical industry: The business of manufacturing medicinal drugs prescribed by a doctor or sold by a chemist

Physiology: The way organs function within the body, for example, the work of the heart, liver and kidneys

Spontaneous generation: The idea that rubbish or decaying material creates microbes (small organisms or germs)

Vaccination: A safe way of stimulating the body's immune system against a particular disease

796
Edward Jenner tested his vaccination for smallpox

801
The first population census in Britain

83
Cholera first arrived in Britain

858
General Medical Act

860
Florence Nightingale published her *Notes on Nursing*

86
Louis Pasteur published his germ theory

865
Elizabeth Garrett Anderson qualified as a doctor

2.2 Were people now living longer?

Learning outcome

By the end of this topic you should be able to:

- understand the effect of changes in industry on medicine and health

Source A: A picture showing a typical industrial town.

As you saw with the Renaissance period, historians find it convenient to use labels for different periods, even though they are not very precise. The term '**Industrial revolution**' is used to describe this period because it was a time of great changes in the way people worked and this led to great changes in the way they lived.

In the mid-18th century various machines were invented that were powered by water or steam and could work more quickly and efficiently than manual workers. The use of machinery in agriculture meant that there was less work to do in the countryside and therefore many people moved to the rapidly growing towns (such as Manchester and Leeds) to work in the new factories. In these towns, the standard of workers' health was usually very poor and disease spread quickly.

- The conditions in the factories led to ill health, for example, poor ventilation created breathing problems.
- There were often accidents in the factories from the machinery.
- The housing in the towns was of poor quality and rooms were damp and poorly ventilated.
- Living conditions were cramped, with a house often containing more than one family.
- Sewers often ran into the rivers where people got their 'clean' water.
- In the big towns and cities there was less access to fresh food than in rural areas.

Activities

1. Look at the tombstones on page 18 showing details taken from a report that was published in 1842. What things can you tell about life expectancy in this period from the details on these tombstones?

2. Look at Source A above and make a list of all the things that would make people unhealthy.

Summary

Poor standards of public health in the industrial towns led to a low life expectancy among workers.

2.3 Killer diseases in Britain, c1750–c1900

Learning outcomes

By the end of this topic you should be able to:

- understand why there was a high mortality rate in industrial towns
- understand why people's ideas about the causes of disease seemed appropriate
- identify elements of continuity between the two periods 1350–1750 and 1750–1900

Cholera

Cholera first arrived in Britain in 1831. Although cholera had been known in India for many centuries, it does not seem to have been present in Britain before this date. It was a frightening disease because people could die within a single day and it spread so quickly that thousands could die within a few weeks.

The picture below is from 1831 and it is about the spread of cholera. It has a similar idea to the Danse Macabre picture of Death in the time of the plague (see page 8) and it is saying that people should spend money on improving the water quality of the Thames or its impurities will kill them.

Source A: The 'Silent Highway'-Man. Your money or your life.

THE "SILENT HIGHWAY"-MAN.
"Your MONEY or your LIFE!"

More information on killer diseases is given in this chart.

Disease	How it is spread	Effects
Cholera	Through bacteria passed on through food and water that have been contaminated by the excreta of an infected person.	Sickness and severe diarrhoea; sufferer dies from dehydration, often within 24 hours. Up to two-thirds of sufferers died.
Diphtheria	Through tiny droplets when coughing and sneezing or through contact with the soiled clothing of an infected person.	Bleeding and sometimes paralysis; suffocation from a blocked throat often leads to death. The death rate was one in ten but it particularly affected children and survivors took a long time to recover.
Smallpox	By touch, or through tiny droplets when coughing or sneezing.	A rash turns into blisters filled with pus; the blisters become crusted and fall off, leaving deep scars. About a third of all sufferers died.
Tuberculosis (TB; also called consumption)	Through tiny droplets when coughing and sneezing.	Coughing becomes constant; victim brings up blood; chest pains; often severe weight loss. Nearly half of all sufferers died.
Typhoid	Through bacteria passed on through food and water that have been contaminated by the excreta of an infected person or through food infected by flies.	Headaches, fever, constipation and then severe diarrhoea. Up to one-third of the sufferers died, especially those who were already weak, such as the old, the young, the malnourished.

What ideas did people have about the causes of disease in the period c1750–c1900?

During the Renaissance there had been a growing interest in science. This affected people's ideas about the causes of disease, and by the 18th century they were less likely to blame disease on supernatural causes or unbalanced humours. People had always been aware that disease spread quickly in dirty, smelly and unhygienic conditions, and so the search for a new explanation of illness based on natural causes now developed into two main theories:

- **miasma**: disease was caused by bad air that was filled with poisonous fumes from rotting matter
- **spontaneous generation**: disease was caused by germs that were produced by flesh and vegetables as they rotted.

ResultsPlus
Build better answers

Why did the authorities find it so difficult to deal with infectious diseases in the 18th and early 19th centuries? (12 marks)

Basic, Level 1 (1–4 marks)
Answer makes general comments about people not understanding how disease was spread.

Good, Level 2 (5–8 marks)
Answer describes the way people tried to deal with infectious diseases, e.g. trying to keep sufferers separate from others, burning barrels of tar or buying medicine from apothecaries.

Excellent, Level 3 (9–12 marks)
Answer explains that until Pasteur's germ theory, they did not understand how diseases spread, therefore any attempt to deal with infectious diseases was unlikely to be effective because it was based on wrong ideas.

Activities

1. In the 18th and early 19th centuries, people still did not know how diseases were spread. Choose one of the killer diseases listed in the table on the opposite page and explain how it could seem to fit the idea of illness caused by:
   a) unbalanced humours
   b) miasma and spontaneous generation.

2. Why did these killer diseases spread so rapidly in an industrial town?

3. Look back at your work on the Black Death. Explain how much progress you think there has been in people's understanding of diseases in the 500 years between the Black Death in 1348 and the first outbreak of cholera in 1831.

Challenge

4. Prepare ten true/false statements about medicine during the industrial revolution that can be done as a revision quiz or as a starter activity for the next few lessons.

Treating cholera

The 'remedies' listed here were all used against cholera in the 19th century:

- burning the clothes and bedding of the dead person
- praying
- cleaning the house and scattering chloride of lime around (this was used in whitewash to make things look clean)
- smoking cigars
- using lucky charms
- burning barrels of tar or vinegar to create smoke in the streets
- making 'special mixtures' of liquids or pills that were supposed to cure all ills.

Summary

Epidemics of infectious diseases killed many people, especially in the towns, where diseases spread quickly. Although diseases such as plague and leprosy had almost died out, new diseases such as cholera, which arrived in Britain in 1831, were extremely frightening.

2.4 The fight against smallpox: Jenner and vaccination

Learning outcomes

By the end of this topic you should be able to:

- understand Jenner's work on vaccination
- explain why he was opposed
- explain the factors that made vaccination successful

If you catch a disease, your body creates special cells called antibodies to fight off the infection and, if you survive, you may become immune to any further attacks of that disease. The fact that some people survived several epidemics of the plague or smallpox was accepted by people throughout history even though they could not explain why it happened. This practical knowledge led to a procedure called **inoculation**, which was developed in China and spread through Asia.

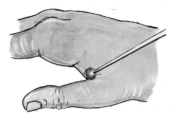

1 A small amount of pus is taken from a sufferer's smallpox blister.

2 It is spread into a small cut made between the thumb and forefinger of the person being inoculated.

3 A mild version of smallpox develops; the person survives and is then immune to further attacks.

Smallpox parties

Lady Mary Wortley Montagu (the wife of the British ambassador to Turkey) witnessed this procedure in Turkey in the early 18th century. She had nearly died from smallpox when she was younger and as she was keen to protect her children she had them inoculated in 1721. The idea quickly became very popular in Britain, and people would even have smallpox parties where they would all be inoculated together. Since doctors were paid for this, they could make a lot of money. However, inoculation did not completely solve the problem of smallpox because not everyone could afford to have it done and inoculation was not always effective or safe.

FASCINATING FACT

Inoculation in Britain was tested on condemned prisoners in 1723.

Activities

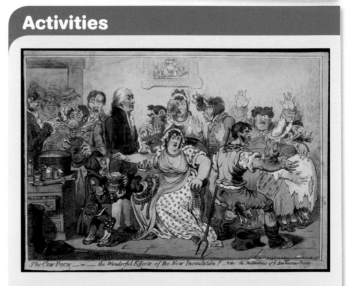

The Cow Pock — or — the Wonderful Effects of the New Inoculation! — vide the Publications of ye Anti-Vaccine Society.

1 Look at the cartoon above carefully. How does it suggest that people did not like the idea of being given cowpox as a vaccination against smallpox?

2 Study the points in the box on Jenner's work on the opposite page and write them out as three lists:

a) one showing all the good points about Jenner's own work

b) one showing all the reasons why there was opposition to Jenner's work

c) one showing outside events that affected Jenner's work.

19th Century News
Doctor from Gloucestershire gets £20k payout

1807

Edward Jenner, a doctor in Gloucestershire, was surprised when local people said they did not need to be inoculated. They claimed that if they had already had cowpox they would not catch smallpox. Jenner decided to check this idea and carried out tests on an eight-year-old boy called James Phipps.

'On 14 May 1796, I took some cowpox matter from a blister on the arm of Sarah Nelmes and inserted it into two cuts I had made on James's arm,' said Jenner. 'A week later he became chilly, lost his appetite and had a headache but the next day he was completely well. On 1 July I inoculated him with smallpox matter but no disease followed. Several months later I tried again, but he still didn't develop even a mild case of smallpox!'

To make absolutely sure of his findings, Jenner vaccinated another 23 people in this way (including his eleven-month-old son) and in 1798 he decided to publish his ideas, giving the name 'vaccination' to his new technique of inoculation with cowpox (because *vacca* is the Latin for cow). However, the Royal Society refused to publish his account and he had to pay for his report to be printed himself. In 1802 the British government awarded Jenner £10,000 for his work against smallpox – and now, five years later, they have given him an additional £20,000.

Jenner's work

- The link only existed between smallpox and cowpox. It did not work for any other diseases.
- Jenner worked in a scientific way and did a number of tests.
- Jenner had pamphlets printed for other scientists to read; the pamphlets described his experiments very clearly so that the other scientists could check his work.
- Vaccination showed that it was possible to prevent some people catching a disease.
- Jenner could not explain how the link between cowpox and smallpox worked.
- Vaccination was not always successful, and some people did develop smallpox because some doctors did not carry out vaccination carefully enough.
- Jenner did not mind other people using his ideas – he wanted lots of people to benefit from his work.
- In 1802 the Jennerian Society was set up in London to promote vaccination and within two years over 12,000 people had been vaccinated.
- When the government provided a grant to pay for people to have free vaccinations, doctors lost money because people no longer paid for inoculations. Therefore many doctors opposed Jenner's work.
- Napoleon in France and President Jefferson in the USA both thought vaccination was a great breakthrough.
- In 1852 the government made it compulsory to be vaccinated.
- When the British government enforced compulsory vaccination in 1872, the number of smallpox cases dropped dramatically, and in 1979 the World Health Organization announced that smallpox had been wiped out completely.

Activities

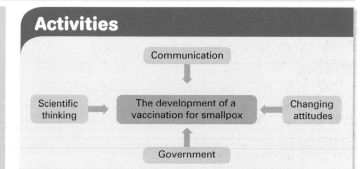

3 The diagram above shows four factors that affected the development of a vaccine for smallpox. Make a copy of this diagram and use the points in the box on Jenner's work to provide examples of the role of each factor.

4 'Individuals and their discoveries are not enough on their own to bring about medical progress.' Explain how far you think this statement applies to Jenner and his work.

Challenge

5 Go back to the list of killer diseases on page 20. Research when a vaccination was successfully discovered for each of them and plot them on a timeline.

Summary

Jenner's discovery of vaccination was an important way of preventing smallpox, but his methods could not be applied to other infectious diseases.

2.5 The development of the germ theory

Learning outcomes

By the end of this topic you should be able to:

- understand how the development of the germ theory was an important breakthrough in the development of vaccines
- understand that new scientific knowledge of disease laid the foundations for later work on the treatment and prevention of disease

The significance of the germ theory

The germ theory – that there are microbes in the air which cause decay – was an important breakthrough in scientific understanding. It disproved the theory of spontaneous generation (see page 21) and led Koch to identify the specific microbes that caused some individual diseases. As a result of this improved understanding of the causes of diseases, scientists hoped they could find ways of treating them. But this was going to take some time, because they would first need to identify the microbe responsible for each separate disease. Only then could there be a cure.

Meanwhile, when Pasteur discovered the technique that created a weakened version of a chicken cholera microbe, almost twenty years later, he realised that vaccines for other diseases could be developed. But this also depended on microbes for each specific disease being identified.

Therefore, despite its importance, this breakthrough in scientific knowledge and understanding had limited impact on medicine at the time because each disease had to be researched individually. Progress in the prevention and treatment of diseases was, therefore, slow.

In the 1850s Louis Pasteur, a French chemist, investigated the problem of liquids turning sour in the brewing and vinegar industries.

↓

More powerful microscopes had recently become available, which meant Pasteur could observe the growth of unwanted small organisms in the liquids.

↓

He discovered heating the liquid killed the bacteria and stopped the liquid going sour.

↓

In 1861 Pasteur published his germ theory, showing that there were microbes in the air and that they caused decay. His work proved the idea of spontaneous generation was wrong because no decay happened if matter was placed in a sealed container. This showed that the microbes causing decay were not produced from the matter itself but were in the air around it.

↓

In 1875, Robert Koch, a German doctor who had read Pasteur's work, decided to investigate whether bacteria were linked to disease. Working with a team of scientists, and funded by the German government, Koch identified the specific microbes that caused the disease anthrax in sheep.

In 1879 Pasteur's team was studying chicken cholera microbes and injecting chickens with the disease. A culture of the bacteria was accidentally left on one side and when it was used, a couple of weeks later, it had become a weakened version, which didn't harm the chickens. Pasteur realised that this could be used as a vaccine to create immunity from that disease for chickens. He called this process 'vaccination' in tribute to the importance of Jenner's work.

↓

Koch identified the microbes causing TB in 1882 and those causing cholera in 1883.

↓

Koch found that chemical dyes could be used to stain specific bacteria so they could be studied more easily under the microscope.

Source A: Pasteur in his laboratory

Scientific experiments

Technology

Recording and communicating results of experiments

The importance of research teams

By the end of the 19th century, scientific research was usually carried out by a team rather than by an individual. A team was more likely to have funding and be able to afford expensive new technology, such as more powerful microscopes. Also, working in a team made it easier to check each other's work and carry out large-scale testing. Furthermore, different members of a team could offer knowledge of different specialisms, for example, medicine, biology and chemistry.

ResultsPlus
Build better answers

What factors affected Pasteur's development of the germ theory? (12 marks)

■ **Basic, Level 1 (1–4 marks)**
Answer makes general comments on the germ theory.

● **Good, Level 2 (5–8 marks)**
Answer describes one factor such as the role of technology leading to improvements in the microscope.

▲ **Excellent, Level 3 (9–12 marks)**
Answer includes some explanation of various factors such as scientific methods or industry and clearly explains how these helped in the development of the germ theory.

Activities

1 Explain why Pasteur called his procedure vaccination even though it is a different technique from Jenner's procedure.

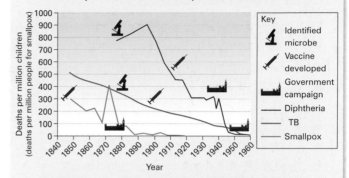

2 Study the graph above, which shows lines for deaths per million children for TB and diphtheria, and adults and children for smallpox. Explain how the graph shows the importance of the following factors on preventing disease at the end of the 19th century:

   a) improvements in scientific knowledge

   b) the role of the government.

3 Why do you think the death rate for TB (indicated by the blue line) was falling even before the vaccine was developed?

4 Why could doctors in the 19th century still not successfully treat illness even after the work of Pasteur and Koch?

5 Why do you think many doctors still recommended regular bloodletting as a preventive measure until the late 19th century?

FASCINATING FACT

As well as bloodletting, purging continued to be used both as a treatment and as a preventive measure. Tobacco vapour or a mixture of water, soap and herbs was used as an enema: it was squirted into the body using a greased pipe.

Summary

Pasteur's germ theory was an important breakthrough in understanding disease and in making it possible to find a way of developing vaccines as a prevention of disease.

2.6 Doctors and training

Learning outcomes

By the end of this topic you should be able to:

- understand the importance of John Hunter's work
- understand the factors affecting changes in doctors' training
- understand that treatment of illness was still very limited even though understanding had improved

FASCINATING FACT

Hunter had an extension built to his house so that he could display all his specimens. Part of the extension had to be open to a height of two storeys so that he could display the stuffed body of a giraffe.

In the medieval and Renaissance periods doctors learned by studying the works of Galen and attending lectures at university. They might have watched a dissection being carried out by the lecturer's assistant but they would not have done one themselves. At the start of the 18th century and the **industrial** period, a doctor's training continued to be mainly theoretical but a small number of criminals' bodies were allowed to be used for dissection in medical schools and hospitals.

Qualifications

Doctors could set up practices once they had been accepted by the Royal College of Surgeons, the Royal College of Physicians or the Society of Apothecaries. Medical training began to improve after 1815 when the Society of Apothecaries and the Royal College of Surgeons introduced examinations before they awarded a certificate. In 1858 the General Medical Act said that a General Medical Council had to be set up and all qualified doctors had to be registered.

However, the fact that doctors could still do relatively little to treat disease meant that they were not always respected.

Practical experience

After Pasteur's germ theory, there was more emphasis on using microscopes and understanding illness, as well as gaining practical experience by observing doctors as they worked in one of the teaching hospitals. Important medical schools developed at Glasgow, Edinburgh, Oxford and London. Once qualified, doctors could apply for a position at a hospital, working under the supervision of an experienced doctor, but they might also volunteer to work at charity hospitals where they would be able to gain more experience. As medical knowledge advanced, doctors tended to divide into general practitioners and those who specialised in specific areas of the body or types of disease – these were usually called consultants.

Dissections

Many medical students recognised the value of dissection and studying the human **anatomy** personally. As a result body snatchers operated in the 18th and early 19th centuries, seizing the bodies of hanged criminals or digging up newly buried corpses in order to provide specimens for students. The most famous of these body snatchers were Burke and Hare, who operated in Scotland. The government tried to end this practice with the Anatomy Act of 1832, which allowed licensed anatomists to take the corpse of anyone dying in the workhouse, who was not claimed by a relative.

Source A: A cartoon titled 'Giving up the Ghost' showing the prosperous doctor unable to prevent Death at the window coming for the poor man's wife.

GIVING UP THE GHOST or ONE TOO MANY.

John Hunter – a scientific approach

Why was Hunter important?

- His lectures on anatomy helped to develop a more professional approach to medical training.
- He emphasised the importance of observation and experiment.
- His students included Edward Jenner, who followed Hunter's methods when investigating cowpox.
- He employed a secretary to write up his notes and paid an artist to draw the discoveries he made through dissection.
- He published several important works, including one about the changes that occurred in pregnancy.

Source B: One of the illustrations from Hunter's work on pregnancy.

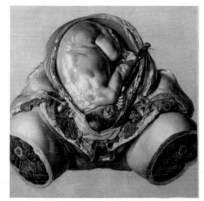

Source C: John Hunter, 1728–1793.

Extremely skilled in the techniques used in dissection, an intensely curious man and a workaholic.

Studied many aspects of anatomy, using specimens to show the human body's structure and **physiology**, the medical problems of conditions like arthritis and also the progressive stages of a disease.

Built up a huge collection of human and animal specimens.

Carried out various experiments as part of a study on the sexually transmitted infections of syphilis and gonorrhoea.

Source D: This picture, by Hogarth, drawn in 1751, shows a scene in a dissecting room at the Surgeon's Hall.

Activities

Improved technology, e.g. thermometer, stethoscope and sphygmomanometer (which measures blood pressure), to diagnose illnesses such as TB or heart conditions

Improved knowledge of disease, e.g. germ theory

What affected the training of doctors?

Improved knowledge of anatomy and physiology, e.g. through dissection

Introduction of medical schools and teaching hospitals

Improved communications, e.g. medical texts, telegrams and phone

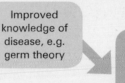

1 Explain the changes that happened in the training of doctors between 1750 and 1900.

2 Look at the ideas map above. Which do you think was the most important aspect of changes in medical training during this period: improvements in knowledge of anatomy and physiology, improved understanding of disease, or improved technology? (Make sure you explain your answer.)

Summary

Major advances were made in knowledge of the body by anatomists like John Hunter, and the scientific approach was now clearly established. However, doctors still had limited ability to treat disease.

2.7 The professionalisation of women in medicine

Changing roles of men and women

From the mid-18th century, there were gradual changes in attitudes towards women in society and by the mid-19th century women began to demand the right to vote and to be able to attend university. Even so, women's role in formal medicine was very limited. Their role in midwifery declined after the invention of forceps in the 17th century because the midwife needed training to use them successfully.

The most famous 'man-midwife' was William Smellie, who moved from Scotland to London in 1739 and would treat poor women for free if his students could attend the birth. His lectures and writings were extremely influential in developing the way childbirth was treated but most ordinary people – who could not afford a trained midwife – continued to use local women with no training but lots of practical experience.

If there was no family member to provide care for a sick person, a nurse might be employed. Although proper training for nurses had begun in Germany, at Kaiserwerth in 1833, nursing was not yet seen as a respectable career in Britain and therefore most nurses were poor and uneducated.

It was not until 1877 that women could qualify as doctors at a British university. Even then, they faced opposition from male students and doctors who thought that women were too emotional for dissections and not intelligent enough for the training, and that patients would not take them seriously.

Source A: Florence Nightingale (1820–1910).

• Came from a wealthy family

• Trained at Kaiserwerth hospital in 1850

• Asked to lead a team of nurses at the military hospital in Scutari during the Crimean War (1854–1856)

• Was initially opposed by the doctors at Scutari

• Worked at a hospital in London from 1853

• Death rate at Scutari fell from 42 per cent to 2 per cent

Source B: Elizabeth Garrett Anderson (1836–1917).

• Came from a wealthy family

• Inspired by feminists in London and by Elizabeth Blackwell, the first woman in the USA to qualify as a doctor

• Repeatedly turned away by medical schools, she worked as a nurse while attending lectures for doctors, until she was forced to stop

• Turned away by medical schools, which refused to accept a woman

• Needed a certificate from one of the three medical organisations to become a doctor – in 1865 she was accepted by the Society of Apothecaries

• Set up a medical practice in London

• Still wanted a medical degree so she learned French and gained the qualification at Paris University

ResultsPlus
Build better answers

Question: Compare the impact for women in medicine of the careers of Nightingale and Garrett Anderson. (12 marks)

■ **Basic, Level 1 (1–4 marks)**
Answers describe the career of one or both women.

● **Good, Level 2 (5–8 marks)**
Answers explain what one or both women did and what impact their work and career had; for example, the Royal Society of Apothecaries was forced to accept Garrett Anderson but then changed their rules so that no other woman could become qualified in the same way.

▲ **Excellent, Level 3 (9–12 marks)**
Best answers will show the impact of the work and career of both women, and will be very clear about the comparison. For example, Nightingale's work had long lasting and widespread results while Garrett Anderson's qualification had a more limited impact but set an important precedent.

Activities

1 What problems faced women who wanted a career in medicine in the 19th century?

2 How much of a breakthrough was it for women that Garrett Anderson eventually became a qualified doctor?

3 Draw an ideas map of factors affecting women in medicine. Colour code them to show:
   a) factors helping women progress
   b) factors holding women back.

Florence Nightingale 1820–1910	Significance
She organised care and supplies at Scutari military hospital, emphasising cleanliness and fresh air (she believed disease was caused by miasma). Her actions contributed to the death rate falling from 42 per cent to 2 per cent.	Her work was reported in British newspapers. The public contributed money that helped establish the Nightingale School for Nurses in London in 1860. She published *Notes on Nursing* about practical care and high standards – which has been translated into 11 languages. She wrote over 200 books about hospital design and organisation. She was also influential in establishing a training school for midwives at King's College Hospital, London in 1861.

Elizabeth Garrett Anderson 1836–1917	Significance
She applied to the Society of Apothecaries (the only one of the three medical bodies that did not state they would not accept women). They refused to accept her but her father took them to court. In 1865 they agreed to register her (but changed their regulations afterwards so that other women could not copy her).	In 1872 she founded the New Hospital for Women in London. In 1874 she helped set up the London School of Medicine for Women. In 1876 an Act of Parliament allowed women to enter medical professions.

Summary

Women's role in medicine continued to be important in the home, but they were now beginning to have a professional role in medicine as both doctors and nurses.

2.8 Hospitals and the care of the sick

Learning outcomes

By the end of this topic you should be able to:

- understand the key aspects of improved provision of care for the sick in this period
- recognise that different social groups received different levels of care
- analyse the extent of change in the provision of care for the sick

Where were people treated?

In 1859, the first cottage hospital opened in Sussex (by 1900 there were 300 of them). This type of hospital was usually small and provided nursing care while the medical treatment was prescribed by the local GPs (general practitioners). At this time there were also 18 voluntary hospitals in London with 4,000 beds. But by and large where you were treated depended on how much money you had.

- The middle and upper classes, who could afford to pay a doctor's fees, would usually be treated at home.
- Some doctors set up sick clubs, where middle- and working-class people could pay a small amount into a fund every week and this would cover any costs if they needed treatment from the doctor.
- The working classes could not pay a doctor and might attend the dispensary or out-patients department of a hospital.
- Many old, sick or disabled people who could not support themselves had to enter the local workhouses, which had been set up by the 1834 Poor Law Amendment Act; in the 1860s there were approximately 65,000 people being cared for in this way.

Public concern about care for the poor

In the 1860s there was a lot of publicity about the level of care offered to poor people. *The Times* newspaper and *The Lancet* medical journal raised concern about the number of old, sick, blind, deaf or disabled people, or those with a mental illness, who were in workhouses intended to support the unemployed poor. Out of 28,550 places in London, only 3,000 of the people in workhouses were actually able bodied unemployed. In 1865 Louisa Twining established the Workhouse Visiting Society, which campaigned for workhouse reform and an improved standard of nursing in the workhouse.

Publicity, pressure and change

This public concern joined with the emphasis in new hospital designs on space and ventilation, to put increasing pressure on local public authorities, such as the Poor Law Unions, to improve the provision of hospital care for the poor.

Source A: Mealtime at the St Marylebone's workhouse, 1900: men's dining room.

Source B: The Birmingham New Poor Law infirmary was opened in 1888. Its pavilion plan, on open ground and with separate isolation wards, is the sort of design that Florence Nightingale promoted.

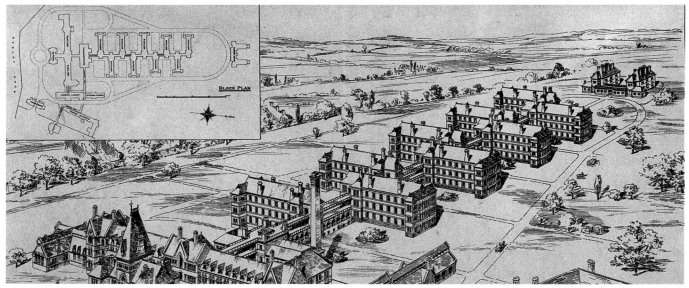

Government action

Starting in London in 1867 but spreading throughout the country, it was ordered that Poor Law Unions should join together to build infirmaries that were separate from the workhouses and that had a full-time doctor appointed to them. The institutions were paid for by local rate-payers. New asylums for the mentally ill and fever houses for people with infectious diseases were also built.

These changes were an improvement but didn't completely separate the workhouse and medical treatment for the poor: in 1887 the Birmingham Poor Law Union built a new infirmary with 1,100 beds, but 1,500 old people were still housed in the workhouse three years later. However, by 1900 the Poor Law infirmaries and the fever hospitals and asylums run by local authorities dealt with far more patients than the voluntary hospitals, and these new infirmaries often went on to become major general hospitals with specialist doctors.

Other factors in the development of hospital care

- Nightingale's work in regulating the training of nurses was a significant factor.
- Pasteur's work on germs also had an impact on hospitals. Joseph Lister began to use carbolic acid to create antiseptic conditions during operations. By 1900 most hospitals accepted the need for antiseptic conditions and equipment in the wards.

Activities

1 Why would a government care about what newspapers or medical journals were saying about medical provision for the poor?

2 At the start of this period there was a big difference in the treatment and care received by the rich and that received by the poor. To what extent did this still exist in 1900?

3 How much progress in the treatment of illness and the care of the sick do you think there was during the period 1750–1900?

4 Draw a diagram to summarise the role of the following four factors in the development of hospital care: publicity; government action; developments in nursing care; and medical advances.

Summary

By 1900 there was the recognition that hospital care needed to be improved. The standard of care within workhouses was rising (although there was still great variation between different areas of the country). However, there was no move yet to fund hospitals from central government.

2.9 Patent medicines and pharmacies

Learning outcomes

By the end of this topic you should be able to:

- understand why people bought patent medicines
- understand how pharmacies developed

During the 19th century there was probably less use made of herbal remedies as people moved away from the countryside, but apothecaries sold many 'preparations', which they advertised as being a cure for practically everything. These preparations took the form of potions, ointments and pills, made from things such as coloured liquids, alcohol, lard, wax, turpentine, ginger and arsenic.

Source A: A scene from 1870, showing people who are waiting to buy medicine from the pharmacist.

> ### FASCINATING FACT
>
> The key ingredient of Godfrey's Cordial, which was often used for babies, was opium. Opium was also used as a cure for flatulence. King George IV used it for insomnia, the Duke of Wellington took it to stay calm, and Florence Nightingale used it for back pain.

The ingredients for pills were made into a paste and then shaped by hand – for rich customers, they might also be covered in gold or silver leaf to make them more attractive and easier to swallow. However, the use of pills in medicine was revolutionised in 1844 when William Brockedon invented a machine to make standardised pills that were produced far more quickly than being made by hand.

Thomas Beecham began selling his pills in 1847 and Jesse Boot, a herbalist from Nottingham, transformed his family shop into a chain of **pharmacies** in the late 19th century. By the end of the 19th century British government regulations stopped many of the harmful ingredients being used in medicine. Meanwhile, the growth of the chemical industry meant that companies such as Wellcome, Boots and Beecham could produce their brand of medicines on a national basis, and they all used advertising in newspapers and posters to increase their sales. This type of business is called the **pharmaceutical** industry.

Other remedies tried in this period:

1   hypnotism

2   magnetism

3   electrical shocks

Influenced by:
• increasing link between science and medicine
• changes in technology and industry (made them available to the public)
• growing interest of the public in new ideas.

Newspaper advertisements/ improved literacy: very important in making ideas acceptable

BUT new treatments mainly used by the middle classes and rich - little change in medicine of ordinary people because of very low incomes.

Source B: These two advertisements from the late 19th century are examples of **patent medicines** that were becoming available, and of the growing pharmaceutical industry.

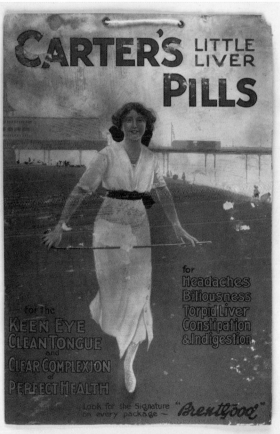

Activities

1   Explain how the role of the apothecary changed into that of a pharmacist during this period.

2   Find examples to show the influence of technology on the development of the pharmaceutical industry.

Summary

The role of the apothecary remained important in offering medicine to ordinary people who could not afford a trained physician. Despite cordials, tonic and pills that claimed to cure all sorts of illnesses, there was still no genuine cure for most diseases or for illnesses such as respiratory or heart problems. However, the pharmaceutical industry grew in importance.

2.10 Change and continuity: how much did medicine change between 1750 and 1900?

The importance of individuals

1 Copy and complete the chart below, comparing the importance of key individuals in this period.

2 Who was the most important of these individuals in bringing about advances in medicine in this period? Explain your answer fully.

3 How far do you think Pasteur's germ theory can be described as a turning point in medicine?

4 Explain why the advances in medicine that were made during the period 1750–1900 could not have been made during the Middle Ages or the Renaissance period.

	Jenner	Pasteur	Koch
What did they do?			
What effect did it have on medicine or treatment at the time?			
What was the long term effect of their work?			
What factors were involved?			

Review

5 Look back to the end of the medieval and Renaissance section of this book on pages 14 and 15. In the review work, you were asked to sort key points into two lists, showing points leading to progress and points that held back developments in medicine.

Use those ideas to do your own review of medicine in the period 1750–1900.

Changes in hospitals

The Great Ormond Street Hospital for sick children was opened in 1852 and contained only ten beds. The picture – from 1856 – shows how the first ward tried to recreate a home atmosphere, but by the time of the new ward in the second picture – built in 1875 – the emphasis was on medicine as a science and a professional approach to the design of hospital wards and to nursing care.

Source A: Great Ormond Street Hospital in 1856.

6 Explain how the changes shown in the pictures of the ward in Great Ormond Street Hospital reflect the changing approaches to medicine in the period 1750–1900.

7 What factors do you think were important in influencing these changes?

Resistance to change

You have already seen that there was resistance to Jenner's vaccination against smallpox, both within the medical profession and from the public. For this reason, advances in medicine were sometimes slow to reach ordinary people. However, the role of the newspaper and the development of photographs meant that people became more aware of problems, and public pressure sometimes forced change

to happen more quickly. You can see this in the concern about the poor in the late-19th century and the moves to improve care of the sick.

8 Look at the points below. Give examples from the period 1750–1900 to show how each of these could be a factor holding back change helping to promote change, or both!
   a) communication and publicity of new ideas
   b) education and training of medical professionals
   c) government action (or lack of it)
   d) finance
   e) general attitudes to new ideas
   f) religious or social beliefs
   g) the working classes getting the vote in 1867 and 1884.

Source B: Great Ormond Street Hospital in 1875.

Wooden floors for easy cleaning

Tidy and orderly appearance

Clean sheets

Big windows for light and ventilation

Nurses have a central role on the ward; they are in uniforms, including caps

Parents and visitors are not required to help with patient care and visiting is now restricted

Summary

There were some significant developments in medicine between 1750 and 1900 but there were also many elements of continuity.

2.11 The work of the historian: statistics

It is tempting to think that statistics are totally reliable, especially when the figures look very precise. However, historians must treat them in the same way as they use all sources and ask the following questions.

1 Who produced the source?

2 Why did they produce the source?

3 Where did they get their information from?

4 Can it be assumed that any information and conclusions based on these figures also applies to other areas in the country?

In 1665, when there was an epidemic of the plague in London, women were employed as searchers to record the number of the dead. If someone had died from the plague, their whole family was locked into the house for 28 days to prevent them spreading the plague any further.

Source A: Bill of mortality for the week beginning 15 August 1665.

Abortive 5
Aged 43
Ague 2
Apoplexie 1
Bleeding 2
Burnt in his bed by a candle at St Giles Cripplegate 1
Canker 1
Childbed 42
Chrisomes 18
Consumption 134
Convulsion 64
Cough 2
Dropsie 33
Feaver 309
Flox and smallpox 5

Frighted 3
Gowt 1
Grief 3
Griping in the guts 51
Jaundies 5
Imposthume 11
Infants 16
Killed by a fall from the Belfry at Allhallows the Great 1
Kingsevil 2
Lethargy 1
Palsie 1
Plague 7165
Rickets 17
Rising of the Lights 11
Scowring 5

Scurvy 2
Spleen 1
Spotted Feaver 101
Stillborn 17
Stone 2
Stopping of the stomach 9
Strangury 1
Suddenly 1
Surfeit 49
Teeth 121
Thrush 5
Timpany 1
Tissick 11
Vomiting 3
Winde 3
Wormes 15

Christened { Males 95, Females 81, In all 176 }   Buried { Males 4095, Females 4202, In all 8297 }   Plague 7165

Increased in the Burials this Week 607
Parishes clear of the Plague 4
Parishes Infected 126

Activities

1 Find three examples of diseases listed in Source A that could also have been the plague.

2 Why might the searcher not have listed the cause of death accurately even if it really was caused by the plague?

3 Find at least one other example of something listed as a cause of death which you feel is not accurate. Can you think why it has been recorded that way?

4 Samuel Pepys lived in London and kept a diary of his experiences during the 1660s. He wrote on 30 August 1665 that the parish clerk had said out of every nine people who died of the plague, he only recorded six plague deaths. Using this information and Source A, what do you think the accurate total of plague deaths could have been for this week in August?

5 Pepys also said that the poor died in such numbers that they were not always recorded. Does that mean that Source A is of no use to historians? Explain your answer.

Before the 19th century population details were not very accurate. Most priests kept records of births and deaths but this information was not sent to any central government office. Many of these records have not survived because the papers have been damaged or simply lost. However:

- In 1801 the government ordered every parish to send in details about the number of houses and the number of families in their area, the number of christenings, marriages and burials, and whether people were employed. This is a census.
- In 1821 the census added people's age.
- In 1841 the census also added gender and occupation.

Other useful information comes from local authorities who began to employ Medical Health Officers who sent annual statistics to central government. You can see from the table that the information tells us the age of death for each person, their gender and what they died from.

Activities

6 Why might you expect the figures given in Source B to be more accurate than the figures in Source A?

7 Why might the figures in Source B still not be totally accurate?

8 Even if Source B is mainly accurate, it does not give us the full picture. For example, a patient might be weakened so much by an illness that they then die from something like bronchitis and pneumonia.

a) Think of three questions you would like to ask about Source B.

b) Explain what other sources of information you would need to consult in order to find out your answers.

9 What different types of sources would you use if you were going to research the history of your local hospital? For each source explain why it would be useful and what limitations it could have.

Source B: The table shows deaths in Maidstone in 1889.

TABLE OF DEATHS during the year 1889, in the Urban Sanitary District of Maidstone		DEATHS FROM ALL CAUSES						DEATHS FROM SPECIFIED CAUSES										
	Estimated to middle 1889	At all ages	Under 5	5 and under 15	15 and under 25	25 and under 60	60 and upwards		Smallpox	Measles	Diphtheria	Typhoid	Diarrhoea and Dysentery	Cholera	Bronchitis, Pneumonia and	Heart disease	Injuries	All other diseases
EAST MAIDSTONE Males	15,422	113	47	9	3	26	28	Under 5	6	2		4			5		4	26
								5 upwards		1					13	6	4	42
Females		120	52	8	4	15	41	Under 5	9	1		3			7	2	2	28
								5 upwards		1	2				9	9	2	45
Total		233																
WEST MAIDSTONE Males	14,201	107	50	5	10	19	23	Under 5	4	5		3			7		1	30
								5 upwards		5					6	4	10	32
Females		110	41	13	4	21	31	Under 5	1	6		1			6	1		26
								5 upwards		7	1	1			15	8		37
Total		217																
Totals	29,623	450	190	35	21	81	123	Under 5	20	14		11			25	3	7	110
								5 upwards		1	15	1	1		43	27	16	156

3.1 Medicine and treatment c1900 to present day: introduction

This section begins with a quick overview of the enormous changes that happened in the 20th century before examining these changes and the reasons for them in more detail. The key words on this page are important throughout this section so you may need to refer back to this page until you understand what they mean!

FASCINATING FACT

The NHS currently takes up about a quarter of all government spending, and is the largest employer in Europe and the third largest employer in the world.

Before…

The rapid industrial changes in the 19th century caused a new set of health problems for the working class, but science and technology also helped to create a better understanding of disease and provided some ways to prevent disease spreading. The government became more involved in dealing with health and disease but the standards of health care still tended to depend upon people's ability to pay.

After…

As the cost of the NHS (National Health Service) continues to rise, there is great debate about the role of government and private health schemes in health care provision. Developments in science and technology have raised hopes of cures for many diseases and conditions but have also led to a debate about ethics within medicine, especially in genetic and embryo research.

ResultsPlus

Watch out!

Many students assume that modern medicine is a story of continual progress but this is not always the case. You will study an example of this on pages 52–53.

Antibiotics: Drugs that stop infections caused by bacteria

Consultant: A doctor specialising in a specific disease or part of the body; usually based in hospital and seeing patients referred by a GP

Crystallography: Using radiation to take a high-power X-ray photograph

DNA: The abbreviation for deoxyribonucleic acid, which contains the genetic instructions for every cell in your body

General practitioner (GP): A doctor who works in a practice dealing directly with the public

Genetics: The study of genes and inherited characteristics

Magic bullet: A chemical drug that kills the microbes causing a specific disease without harming the rest of the body

National Health Service (NHS): An organisation set up by the government in 1948 to give free health care to all

Prescription charges: Payment for medicine that has been prescribed by a doctor

Radiotherapy: The use of radiation in medicine, often to attack cancer

 91
National Insurance introduced

919
Nursing Act

1941
Mass production of penicillin began

 948
The establishment of the NHS in Britain

 953
Watson and Crick show the structure of DNA

2003
Human Genome Project completed

3.2 Why did life expectancy increase in the 20th century?

Learning outcome

By the end of this topic you should be able to:

● understand some of the reasons why life expectancy increased during the 20th century

At the start of the 20th century, photographs, film, electricity, the bicycle and the motor car had all been invented but many people continued to live and work in cramped and unhygienic conditions, using oil lamps or gas lighting. Despite medical advances many people would simply not be able to afford to see a doctor and the average life expectancy in 1901 was only 47. Pasteur's germ theory had led to a range of vaccinations being developed but there had been little progress in the search for a way to cure diseases and most medicines were still based on mixtures of ingredients such as plants and spices.

The 20th century was a story of huge improvements in the treatment of illness. Most people in the UK now have better living standards than in the 19th century, and often better diets as a result of our increased prosperity. We also tend to assume that even if we don't have a cure for an illness now, science will probably find one in the future, and we can successfully treat far more health problems, such as heart conditions.

Activities

A drawing showing the living conditions of families in slum housing in the early 1900s.

1 What clues are there in the above picture to suggest that there was a low standard of living among the poor at the start of the 20th century?

2 The two charts on this page are comparing the main causes of death in 1900 with the main causes of death in 1997.

   a) What were the three main causes of death in 1900?

   b) What were the three main causes of death in 1997?

   c) Why do you think the main causes of death changed during the 20th century?

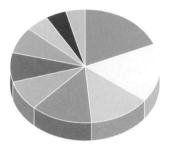

Main causes of death in 1900

- Tuberculosis
- Pneumonia / influenza
- Diarrhoea
- Heart disease
- Liver disease
- Injuries
- Strokes
- Cancer
- Bronchitis
- Diphtheria

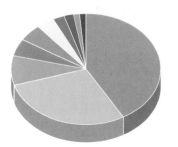

Main causes of death in 1997

- Heart disease
- Cancer
- Stroke
- Chronic lung disease
- Unintentional injuries
- Pneumonia / influenza
- Diabetes
- Suicide
- Chronic kidney disease
- Chronic liver disease

Summary

- In 1900 poor standards of living and a limited ability to treat illness meant that life expectancy was still low.

- The 20th century saw great improvements, which had a major effect on life expectancy.

3.3 Developments in the fight against disease

Learning outcomes

By the end of this topic you should be able to:

- understand the development of vaccinations
- understand the factors involved in the development of magic bullets to cure disease
- understand the significance of the development of magic bullets in finding cures for diseases

Vaccination timeline

1896	Typhoid
1906	Tuberculosis
1913	Diphtheria
1927	Tetanus
1952	Whooping cough
1954	Polio
1964	Measles
1988	MMR (Measles, Mumps, Rubella)

Cause and prevention of disease

Earlier in this book (pages 24–25) you saw how Pasteur's germ theory was an important breakthrough in understanding the causes of many diseases. You also saw how the work of Pasteur and Koch led to the development of vaccinations to prevent disease, which is summarised here.

Scientists in Europe find the way to develop chemical cures for illness

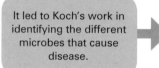

| Pasteur's germ theory in 1861 was an important breakthrough in understanding how disease is spread. | It led to Koch's work in identifying the different microbes that cause disease. | The technique to prevent people from catching a disease was developed and applied to more and more diseases. | The government also began to intervene more in people's lives. They first encouraged and then later insisted that all children were vaccinated. |

Improved understanding of the causes of disease also led to a search for '**magic bullets**' that would *cure* diseases.

The first magic bullet

- *Emil von Behring developed Koch's work to isolate the antitoxins used by the body to fight diphtheria – then found a way to inject them to cure the disease.*
- *Paul Ehrlich (a member of Koch's team) now set up his own research team to build on this work. Ehrlich knew certain dyes stained specific microbes (Koch's work) and antitoxins only attacked the disease microbes (Behring's work).*
- *Ehrlich tried to combine a dye with other chemicals to find a cure for syphilis – a 'magic bullet' that would only target the disease microbe and not harm the rest of the body.*
- *Ehrlich researched for several years (only possible because he received government funds).*
- *In 1909 Dr Sahachiro Hata joined the research team and reviewed some previous experiments. Hata discovered there had previously been a mistake – the 606th compound that they had tested and dismissed was actually effective!*
- *This treatment was called Salvarsan 606.*
- *The use of chemical drugs to target and cure illness was an important breakthrough.*

Source A: A poster advertising immunisation.

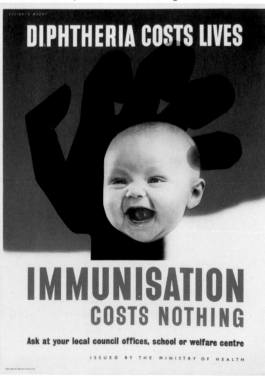

The second magic bullet

It was not until 1932 that a second magic bullet was found when Gerhard Domagk discovered that a particular red dye was effective against some cases of blood poisoning and he developed the drug Prontosil. Many people died after simple cuts or scratches became infected, so this cure for blood poisoning could save many lives.

Research showed that the key ingredient in Prontosil was sulphonamide (a chemical compound) and other sulphonamide drugs were developed that could cure pneumonia, scarlet fever and meningitis.

These discoveries were important because medicine could now cure many of the infections and diseases that had previously led to death. At first, treatment tended to be by injection, but the developments in technology in the late 19th century had made it possible to mass-produce pills and now the pharmaceutical industry began to grow rapidly.

FASCINATING FACT

Domagk's daughter pricked her finger on a needle and was dying from blood poisoning. He had not tested Prontosil on humans, only on mice, but he risked using it – and saved her life.

Activities

1 Copy and complete the flow chart below to show the different stages in the development of magic bullets.

Behring's work showed that …

⬇

Ehrlich's research showed that …

⬇

Hata showed that …

⬇

Magic bullets were an important medical breakthrough because…

Activities

2 Use the information in this section to explain how the science of chemistry helped in the development of medical cures.

3 Draw an ideas map to show the different factors affecting the discovery of magic bullets.

4 Explain how the discovery of magic bullets can be seen as a turning point for medicine in the 20th century.

Challenge

5 Design a page about magic bullets for a website on the history of medicine. Your website page should include each of the following:

- a timeline
- a picture of a famous person involved in the development of magic bullets
- an explanation of each stage in the work
- an explanation of why this work was important
- a diagram to support some of your comments
- links to other website pages.

ResultsPlus

Watch out!

Be careful to avoid confusing the terms vaccination and cure.

Summary

Scientific research led to a better understanding of the individual microbes that cause disease. Communication between scientists in different countries led to various vaccines being developed to prevent people becoming ill. There was also the discovery of 'magic bullets' (a way of using chemicals to target and kill specific microbes), which created the first synthetic cure for many diseases.

3.4 Alexander Fleming and the development of penicillin

Learning outcomes

By the end of this topic you should be able to:

- understand the work of Fleming and of Florey and Chain in the discovery of penicillin
- understand the factors involved in the discovery of penicillin
- evaluate the roles played by Fleming and by Florey and Chain in the discovery of penicillin

FASCINATING FACT

Fleming did not actually make a new discovery – there are records from the Middle Ages, and even earlier, of people using mouldy bread to fight infection even though they didn't understand why. There is also a record of a doctor called Joseph Lister using penicillin to fight infection in a patient in 1871.

Alexander Fleming was a chemist working at St Mary's Hospital in London. In 1928 he noticed that a culture of bacteria growing in a Petri dish was being attacked and killed by an unknown mould growing in the same dish.

This ruined his experiment but he decided to research the mystery killer mould before throwing it away. He discovered that it was an excellent antibiotic, penicillin, but he only tested it on bacteria in the laboratory, not on bacteria in living organisms.

Fleming published his findings in 1929 but he was unable to get funding to develop his work so he returned to his original research.

It was difficult to produce pure penicillin and so it did not seem practical to try to use it in medicine. However, Howard Florey and Ernst Chain, two scientists working in Oxford, read about Fleming's research and in 1939 they set up a team including a range of specialists to develop penicillin.

In 1940 they tested it on mice, and in 1941 they conducted tests on a patient. The test showed that penicillin acted like a miracle drug on people who were dying from infection. Unfortunately, there was only a small amount of penicillin available and the patient died when the penicillin ran out.

Florey became determined to develop the mass production of penicillin but it could not be synthesised from chemicals (like Salvarsan 606 or Prontosil). The mould had to be cultured on a broth and exposed to air in order to grow. This meant that they had to use a collection of containers, including baths, bedpans, milk churns and food tins, and had to hire six assistants just to deal with this stage of the work. No British firm was able to create the technology needed to mass produce penicillin – partly because many factories were being damaged by the bombing raids during the Second World War or were already working to full capacity producing other drugs needed during the war.

Florey refused to patent penicillin, believing it should be available for everyone, and in June 1941 Florey and Norman Heatley (another member of the team) went to the USA to see if drug companies there would fund their research. At first they were unsuccessful but in December 1941 the USA entered the Second World War and

the US government was now prepared to fund the mass production of penicillin. They knew that in war many soldiers were likely to die from infection rather than from actual injuries and so mass-produced penicillin could save many lives.

Florey had discovered that drying the mould at low temperatures was the most successful method of purifying penicillin. Scientists at the chemical company Pfizer, in New York, used an old ice-cream freezer to develop a method of freeze-drying that was eventually used for large-scale production in 1944.

Activities

1 Create a timeline for the discovery and mass production of penicillin 1871–1944. On your timeline, colour code the work of
   a) Fleming and
   b) Florey and Chain.

2 How fair do you think it was that when a Nobel Prize was awarded for the discovery of penicillin, it was given jointly to the three men, Fleming, Florey and Chain? Explain your answer.

3 Complete the following diagram showing the role of factors in the development of penicillin.

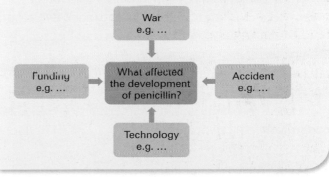

ResultsPlus
Build better answers

Why did it take so long for penicillin to be mass produced? (12 marks)

■ **Basic, Level 1 (1–4 marks)**
Answer makes general comments about the production of penicillin.

● **Good, Level 2 (5–8 marks)**
Answer describes the different stages in the production of penicillin, showing the work of Fleming and the work of Florey and Chain.

▲ **Excellent, Level 3 (9–12 marks)**
Answer identifies reasons why Fleming did not develop the mass production of penicillin and explains how Florey and Chain overcame the problems.

Summary

The development of an antibiotic that could cure bacterial disease and infection was a major advance in medicine. The use of natural organisms to fight bacteria was effective in many cases where chemical drugs were not and, once penicillin was mass produced, it could save thousands of lives.

3.5 Care of the sick c1900–1948

Learning outcomes

By the end of this topic you should be able to:

- understand the extent of the improvement in medical care during the early 20th century
- understand the key factors affecting these improvements

The early 20th century

At the start of the 20th century, it was still the women in the family who were mainly responsible for treating most illnesses and caring for the sick. Because doctors had to be paid for every visit, people would only use doctors if they were really ill, so most illnesses were treated with patent medicines or preparations bought from a chemist. Traditional 'folk remedies' continued to be used, such as a red cloth to help you recover from a cold or influenza and a sweaty sock tied around the neck to help a sore throat. Minor surgery, such as taking out tonsils, was often done by a doctor on the kitchen table. A **general practitioner (GP)** might also do some minor surgery in a local cottage hospital but anything serious would be referred to a specialist **consultant** in a big hospital.

Source A: A poster advertising Sanatogen tonic, a patent medicine.

Charitable hospitals

Many hospitals offered only basic care for the sick rather than the range of treatments we now expect, but some were aimed at specific groups of people. For example, sanatoriums were built to provide a healthy diet, fresh air and hygienic conditions, which patients with TB needed if they were to recover.

Since many hospitals were funded by charity, effective fundraising was vital. In 1912, Queen Alexandra, the mother of King George V (1910–1936), started a national Rose Day, on which volunteers sold roses to raise money for hospitals. The first Rose Day collected the equivalent of £2 million in today's money.

Source B: An Alexandra Rose Day in 1912.

Source C: The outpatients department of St Paul's Eye Hospital, Liverpool, c1931, showing the problems charities faced in dealing with the number of people who needed help.

Improved access to health care	Improved standard of medical care available
By 1900, most cities had built infirmaries, fever houses and asylums to care for the poor. There were also local cottage hospitals and specialised sanatoriums, although most of these depended on charity for their funding.	Nurses were trained within a hospital.
1907: health visitors were introduced to visit mothers and help them care properly for their new babies.	By 1900 doctors had to have a university medical degree and to be accepted by the General Medical Council. They would have carried out dissections while training and have accompanied a doctor working on the hospital wards. Increasingly, doctors chose to become either a General Practitioner, who treated the community, or a doctor who worked in a hospital, usually specialising in one area of medicine.
1911 National Insurance Act: working men, their employers and the government all paid into a fund to cover doctors' fees and medical costs if a worker became ill, although it only applied to certain groups of men and did not cover their families.	1902 Midwives Act: midwives had to be properly trained and registered (it was hoped this would lower the rate of infant mortality).
	1919 Nursing Act: this set up the General Nursing Council to enforce high standards of training for nurses.

Increasing role for government

During the later part of the 19th century, the government had begun to take more responsibility for the public's health. This change of attitude was reinforced when over a third of the men who volunteered to fight in the British Army in the Boer War (1899–1902) were declared unfit and had to be turned away. Since Britain relied on her army and navy to control a large empire, finding ways of improving the health of the working class became an important issue for the government, and war was therefore a factor in speeding up these changes.

There were improvements in how people could access care as well as improvements in the care available, with several key Acts being passed by the Liberal government in the period 1905–1911 (see table above). However, there were fewer doctors in the poorer areas. Doctors could choose who to accept as their patients and they could refuse to give treatment if the patient could not pay them.

In 1919 the Ministry of Health was set up, which gave the government an overview of health care provision in the whole country. This was an important step in the government taking more responsibility for health, but actual provision continued to be a mixture of people paying for private care, local authorities providing some support and many hospitals relying on funding from charity.

The death of 3,000 children from diphtheria in 1938 shocked the government and led to a vaccination programme offering free immunisation.

FASCINATING FACT

Coca-Cola was originally developed as a patent medicine. The claim was that it would cure all nervous afflictions, sickness, headaches, neuralgia, hysteria and melancholy, among other things.

Activities

1 Make a list of government actions that had a role in improving medical care in the period 1900–1939.

2 Explain why many people continued to use traditional home remedies when more scientific treatment was possible.

Summary

Although the government was taking an increased role in improving the health of the nation, by 1939 there was still no national organisation offering the same level of care to everyone, and access to health care remained patchy.

3.6 The creation of the NHS

Learning outcomes

By the end of this topic you should be able to:

- understand the increasing intervention by the government in providing health care
- understand some of the problems facing the NHS today

Reasons for the NHS being set up

- The government had become increasingly concerned about the inequalities of health care in the early 20th century, especially once women got the vote in 1918.
- The bombing raids in the Second World War (1939–1945) produced many casualties in the cities and the government set up a national Emergency Medical Service. This brought hospitals throughout the country under the control of the Ministry of Health. Some new hospitals and 1000 new operating theatres were built and additional equipment was provided. The hospitals provided free treatment, a blood transfusion service was created and an ambulance service was set up.

The Beveridge report in 1942 identified disease as a problem for the government to deal with after the Second World War. Plans were made for a **National Health Service (NHS)**, which was set up in 1948.

Aneurin Bevan, the Minister for Health, faced huge opposition from doctors who did not want to be organised by the government and were afraid they would be less well paid as part of an NHS.

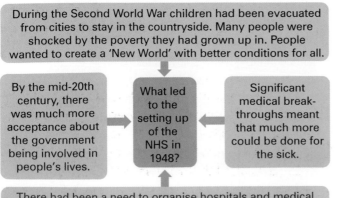

During the Second World War children had been evacuated from cities to stay in the countryside. Many people were shocked by the poverty they had grown up in. People wanted to create a 'New World' with better conditions for all.

By the mid-20th century, there was much more acceptance about the government being involved in people's lives.

What led to the setting up of the NHS in 1948?

Significant medical break-throughs meant that much more could be done for the sick.

There had been a need to organise hospitals and medical staff during the Second World War.

The National Health Service 1948

Taxes were used to pay for a wide range of care offered to people, including:

- the right to see a GP and to be referred to hospital
- treatment by dentists and opticians
- health care for pregnant women and young children
- ambulances and emergency treatment
- health care for the elderly.

This had a major impact on people's health. Previously only those covered by the national insurance system could see a GP free of charge. Non-working women and children were not covered. Although many doctors set up schemes where people paid a small amount every week to cover the cost of treatment when it was needed, many people still could not afford this. The cost of the doctor's visit and the medicine would often make people delay seeking treatment until they were seriously ill. Through the NHS people could see their doctor and get treatment at an early stage of an illness and therefore had a better chance of recovery, and access to professional nursing care. These changes marked a significant improvement in the accessibility of medical care and facilities, and benefited enormously the poorest people in society.

At first all treatments were entirely free, and the government believed the cost of health care would actually go down because so much illness would be prevented. However, the expense of running the NHS was soon much higher than expected and **prescription charges** were introduced in 1951.

Costs

The cost of the NHS is now a major problem for the government, as it increases every year. This is because:

- As people live longer they are more likely to develop problems needing treatment.
- Improvements in medicine mean people expect a greater range of treatment, for example, kidney dialysis, heart surgery, care for premature babies, cancer.
- New drugs can help many conditions but the costs can be very high.

Source A: A modern NHS hospital ward.

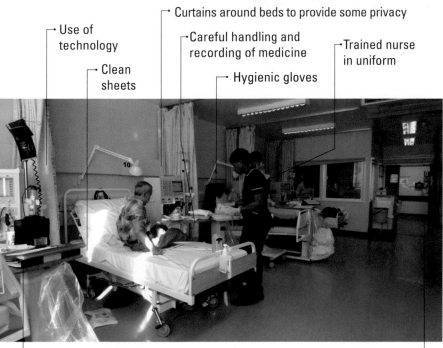

Use of technology

Curtains around beds to provide some privacy

Careful handling and recording of medicine

Trained nurse in uniform

Clean sheets

Hygienic gloves

Patient's medical notes at end of each bed

Visitors limited to control infection

Activities

1 Study Source A, the photograph of a modern hospital ward. How many developments can you identify that show changes since the 19th century, for example:

 a) improved knowledge and understanding of illness?

 b) improved standards of hygiene?

 c) greater use of technology?

2 Write two short articles for a newspaper: one article to celebrate the achievements and successes of the NHS 1948–2008, and another to criticise its shortcomings and disappointments.

3 Use the illustration below showing the different aspects of the NHS. Explain how extensive the role of the NHS is in improving public health.

- Treatment is more complex and equipment more expensive with new technology such as MRI scans.
- Staff costs are high because of increased training for doctors and nurses, increased wages for highly trained staff, and nursing care while patients recover from treatment.

Long waiting lists for treatment developed in the late 20th century and many people's conditions deteriorated before they could get the specialist help they needed. As a result, many people now have some form of private health insurance to cover the cost of treatment.

In recent years GPs have been encouraged to offer a wider range of care, and many now have a nurse attached to their practice and run specialised clinics. However, changes in the way GPs are funded by the state have meant that few of them now offer an emergency service at night or at weekends – this is usually organised by an agency now.

In 2008 the NHS celebrated its 60th anniversary, but there is much discussion about whether it should continue in its current form or if there should be radical changes to the system.

Summary

Only the government had the ability to coordinate a national system and to provide the finances necessary for the system to work. Although there have been significant improvements in health care, this has come at a great cost. The future of the NHS is an area of political debate.

3.7 Training for doctors and nurses

Learning outcomes

By the end of this topic you should be able to:

- understand the changes in the training of doctors and nurses since 1900
- understand the significance of the changes in training since 1900

As you have already seen on pages 31–32 there were significant changes in medical training during the 18th and 19th centuries. During the Renaissance period, the Church had lost its control of medical training, and in the 18th century students began to learn from direct observation rather from the works of Galen. They began to carry out dissections and then, in the 19th century, to study microbes under the microscope. Also in the 19th century, the General Medical Council was set up to control the profession and women gradually became accepted as doctors. Meanwhile, nurses had more formal training, introduced by Florence Nightingale.

Training doctors in the 20th century

At the start of the 20th century, doctors had to qualify and then register with the General Medical Council, but then they could set up their practices anywhere they wanted and choose which patients to accept. Many opened practices in middle or upper class areas where they could be sure of getting patients. Some would set up in poorer areas and were willing to treat people who paid into a local sickness club. However, there was little specialisation and there were also limited opportunities for doctors to receive any further training.

During the 20th century, as knowledge of disease and various conditions increased, and especially after the NHS was set up, many doctors in hospitals specialised much more than previously. GPs also became much more conscious of the need to update their knowledge and to understand new developments. Articles in medical journals, conferences and the Internet have all helped to professionalise the training of medical personnel.

Doctors

Training now takes about seven years, including:

- taking a university degree
- spending time in hospitals, gaining experience in a range of areas and gradually taking more responsibility
- becoming a GP or working with a consultant in a hospital and developing a specialist area.

Paramedics

As research provides new information on treatment and prevention, appropriate training is rolled out throughout the NHS. For example, scientific research has shown that quick medical intervention is particularly important in cases of heart attack or stroke. As a result, paramedics are now trained to assess a patient and take action whenever possible before they take them to hospital.

Source A: In the 20th century, nurses' training meant they had a better understanding of the range of treatments available to patients.

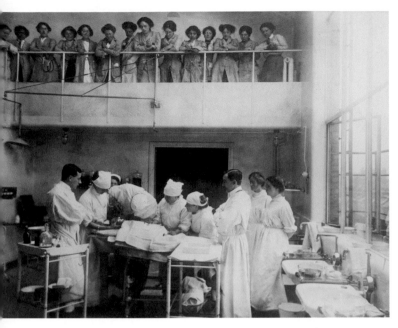

Source B: Total number of doctors in England in 2004, including GPs and those working in hospitals, from consultant, the highest level, to house officer, the lowest level.

England	Total	Male	Female
All staff	107,232	67,107	40,125
GPs	34,885	20,366	14,519
Consultants	30,650	22,835	7,815
Registrar group	16,823	10,234	6,589
Senior house officers	20,601	11,702	8,899
House officers	4,273	1,970	2,303

FASCINATING FACT

The Royal College of Nurses only allowed men to become registered nurses in 1939.

Nurses

Training for nurses is a mixture of academic work and practical experience.

- Nurses must hold a degree or diploma in nursing, which takes three years.
- They must be registered with the Nursing and Midwifery Council.
- They receive practical training working on a range of wards and in specialised situations.
- They must pass further exams before they can administer drugs or chemotherapy.

Activities

1 What do you think has been the most significant change in the training of doctors in the period between the Renaissance in the 16th century and the 20th century?

2 Source B demonstrates that in the 21st century, women make up over one-third of the medical profession; what do you notice about the proportion of female to male doctors at each level?

3 What does Source B suggest about the 'breakthrough' effect of the achievement of Elizabeth Garrett Anderson?

4 Looking at the figures in Source B, how do you think these statistics might have changed by the year 2020?

5 Think about the 'Fascinating fact' on this page; what does this suggest about attitudes towards nursing as a profession?

Summary

Health care provision significantly improved in the 20th century with the emergence of a welfare state and the increased professionalism of doctors and nurses.

3.8 The discovery of the double helix and the genetic revolution

Learning outcomes

By the end of this topic you should be able to:

- to understand that the discovery of DNA helped scientists to understand genetic illness
- understand the significance of the discovery of the DNA structure in creating the potential for future medical treatment
- understand the relative importance of the factors involved in the discovery of DNA and its future potential in medical treatment

Background

- Study of **genetics** began in the 19th century, when Mendel showed how characteristics can be passed down from one generation to the next.
- During the 20th century, scientists could take photographs of human cells through two improvements in technology – electron microscopes and X-rays (using a technique called **crystallography**).
- It became known that each cell in the body contains DNA, which is the set of codes controlling the genes that decide eyes and hair colour, height, and so on.
- If scientists could work out how these genetic codes fitted together in a **DNA** strand, they might be able to identify which genes were responsible for inherited conditions (such as sickle cell anaemia and cystic fibrosis) or conditions such as Down's syndrome.

Francis Crick and James Watson, two Cambridge scientists, worked together to investigate the structure of DNA. Crick was a physicist and Watson a chemist, but their work also made use of X-ray crystallography by Maurice Wilkins and Rosalind Franklin at King's College Hospital in London. In fact, it was one of Franklin's photographs that suggested that genes were arranged in a double helix structure.

Source A: The double helix structure of DNA.

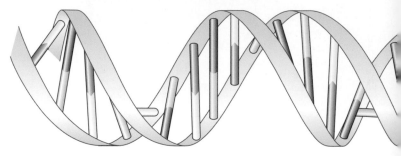

DNA opens the door to new cures for genetic conditions!

1953 Crick and Watson discovered the structure of DNA.

1990 The Human Genome Project, led by Watson, set out to map the location of every single one of the 30,000–35,000 genes in the 23 chromosomes in every cell of the human body.

The project involved hundreds of scientists working in 18 teams. The first draft was produced in 2000.

Scientists have identified certain genes that pass on specific hereditary conditions.

There are new techniques for skin grafts, better production of insulin for diabetics, and better vaccines.

There is a better understanding of conditions such as Down's syndrome and leukaemia, and whether people are more likely to develop certain forms of cancer.

The result

There has been further research to develop techniques to alter faulty genes within the body and prevent genetic illnesses from developing.

The discovery has been made that stem cells (found in the bone marrow of long bones and the pelvis) can transform into various types of cells used around the body – which offers a chance of replacing faulty cells with healthy ones.

Research into genetic conditions requires very specialised knowledge and expensive, high-tech equipment, but it offers exciting possibilities. The diagram shows some of the areas of current research.

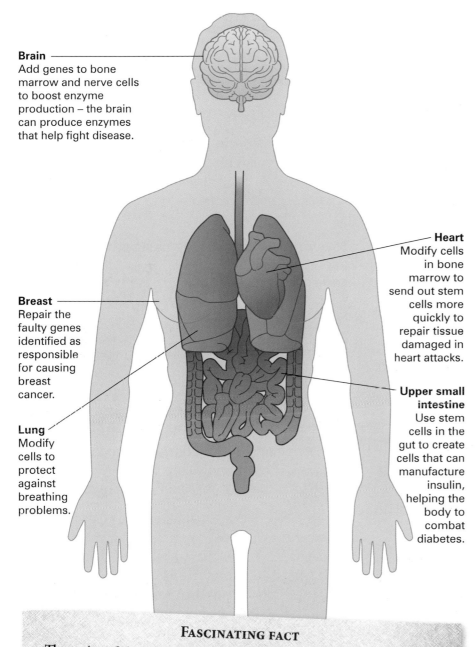

Brain
Add genes to bone marrow and nerve cells to boost enzyme production – the brain can produce enzymes that help fight disease.

Breast
Repair the faulty genes identified as responsible for causing breast cancer.

Lung
Modify cells to protect against breathing problems.

Heart
Modify cells in bone marrow to send out stem cells more quickly to repair tissue damaged in heart attacks.

Upper small intestine
Use stem cells in the gut to create cells that can manufacture insulin, helping the body to combat diabetes.

FASCINATING FACT
The order of the genes within the DNA strand is unique for every single human, except identical twins. For this reason, DNA testing is used to establish the relationship between people, and can be used by the police to identify individuals.

Activities

1 Look at Source A opposite. Explain the roles played by science, technology and communication in the discovery of DNA structure.

2 Research – find out about recent developments in genetic medical research, for example embryo research, genetic screening, or the attempts to 'fix' faulty genes.

3 How do you think students in a hundred years will view these early stages of genetic treatment?

- As a turning point where humans discovered the secret to end all disease?

- As an important stage in the development of medicine (like the germ theory)?

Or is there a chance that it will not lead to new discoveries (like Jenner's vaccinations)?

Summary

The discovery of the structure of DNA by Crick and Watson made use of a wide range of specialist knowledge. Further research improved our understanding of genetic conditions and now scientists are beginning to use that knowledge in order to treat and prevent those conditions.

3.9 The role of science and technology in medicine during the 20th century

Learning outcomes

By the end of this topic you should be able to:

- understand the way science and technology have contributed to medical advances in the 20th century
- understand that science and technology have not always led to progress within medicine
- evaluate the role played by science and technology within medicine in the 20th century

The benefits of science

In the 20th century, scientific research and knowledge has led to:

- chemical treatment of disease (magic bullets)
- **antibiotics**, which used living organisms to fight disease
- more vaccines to prevent the spread of disease
- a better understanding of genetics: genetic changes that cause problems and genetic changes that can help
- treatments being developed for conditions, such as diabetes, which were previously incurable.

Blood transfusions

In the past, most attempts at transfusions had led to the death of the patient, but in 1901 Karl Landsteiner discovered that there were four different blood groups, and transfusions were only successful if the donor's and patient's blood groups were the same.

This discovery meant that:

- people who might die from losing a lot of blood could now be kept alive
- people with blood disorders (such as anaemia) could receive treatment.

The only problem was that blood could not be stored (it clotted), so the donor and the patient had to be together, for the transfusion to be carried out. The high number of injuries during the First World War (1914–1918) sped up the search for a solution.

In 1915 it was discovered that adding sodium citrate prevented blood from clotting, but the blood cells soon deteriorated. In 1916, new scientific techniques made it possible to store blood for longer periods to establish blood banks.

Source A: Different blood groups stored ready for transfusion.

Problems of science and technology

New technologies do not always have the effects intended – or sometimes the side effects may be worse than the original condition being treated.

For example, in the 1960s a new drug called thalidomide was used to prevent morning sickness in pregnant women but it was found that it affected the growth of the unborn baby, and in particular, the development of the arms and legs (see the photo below).

Source B: A child effected by thalidomide.

An aid to research

The powerful electron microscope was invented in 1931. Later, X-ray crystallography was developed, which was even more powerful. You have already seen how that played a role in the discovery of the structure of DNA.

An aid to diagnosis or monitoring of illness

- Technology can be used to scan a patient and diagnose internal problems.
- Endoscopes – a flexible tube containing a camera – can be passed inside the body.
- Nuclear medicine – radioactive elements can be injected into the bloodstream to help track what is happening inside the body.

Source C: Incubators help keep premature babies alive.

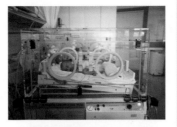

The benefits of technology

Source D: An MRI scan showing a brain tumour.

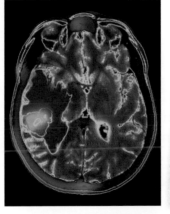

An aid to treatment

- X-rays were discovered by Roentgen in 1895, and by 1902 people realised that they could be used to 'burn' and shrink tumours in a technique called **radiotherapy**.
- Pacemakers and kidney dialysis machines keep people alive when their heart or kidneys are not functioning properly.
- Hypodermic needles and intravenous drips help to give a precise dose of medicine.

An aid for people to monitor their own health

Kits for people to test their own blood pressure or for diabetics to test their blood sugar levels help people to stay healthy.

FASCINATING FACT

Ultrasound scans, which are used to study the unborn baby in the womb, are based on sonar technology and were originally used by submarines.

As well as concerns about the side effects of new drugs, there is a lot of debate about whether scientists should 'play God' and use their knowledge of genetics to change people's bodies. Some research depends on experiments with human embryos; others combine animal and human cells together; and cloning has already been used on animals. The medical potential of these experiments is colossal – but many people object to them on religious and moral grounds or from fear that the side effects could be equally far reaching.

Activities

1. Overall, how much do you think science has helped medicine to progress since 1900?
2. What do you think is the most important aspect of technology:
   - supporting research in understanding disease
   - helping to diagnose and monitor a condition
   - treating illness?
3. Why might people's attitudes towards science hold back developments in medicine?
4. Why does so much research depend on charity funding?

Summary

Advances in scientific knowledge have had a huge effect on medicine in the 20th century but they rely on developments in technology. People have very different attitudes towards the relationship between science and medicine.

3.10 Change and continuity: how much has medicine changed since 1900?

Learning outcome

By the end of this topic you should be able to:

- to understand that changes happen at different rates

How change happens

Many factors have led to changes in medicine, and they often act in combination. For example, some developments in science and technology happen only because the government is prepared to fund them.

Factors can have both positive and negative effects. For example, war provides opportunities to experiment and speeds up some developments – the First World War gave an added urgency to the search to find a way to store blood because it would save many injured soldiers who needed transfusions. However, war can hold back other developments because it diverts money and research away from work that is less obviously relevant (see pages 42–43).

Speed of change

You should also remember that changes happen at different speeds. One scientific or technological breakthrough can lead to several others in a very short space of time, such as happened with the rapid developments in vaccines or genetics. Yet these discoveries can take a long time to have an effect on the treatment people receive.

1990	Human Genome Project was launched – an international effort to map all of the genes in the human body.
1994	The first breast cancer gene was discovered.
1995	The discovery of a gene linked to Parkinson's disease led to hope of future treatment and a cure for this condition.
1996	Scottish scientists created a sheep named Dolly using cells cloned from an adult sheep.
1997	The discovery was made that stem cells can be used for repairs to damaged or faulty tissues in the body.
1998	A rough draft of the human genome map was produced, showing the locations of more than 30,000 genes.

Source A: Dolly the sheep died after six years, half the usual life expectancy of this breed of sheep. She was then stuffed and put on display at the Royal Museum of Scotland.

Change and progress

When antibiotics were discovered it was thought that infection had been completely conquered, but some types of bacteria have become resistant to these drugs. The 'superbugs' MRSA and C. difficile have caused deaths in some British hospitals in the early 21st century, and this has led the British government to insist on new standards of hygiene in the NHS. Scientists have also been working on new methods to combat these infections. This example shows us that progress in medicine is sometimes slow and not as complete as we believe it is.

Source B: Visitors to hospitals are reminded of the importance of hygiene to prevent the spread of diseases such as MRSA.

'Alternative' medicine

Partly as a reaction to some of the problems of science, there has also been a move towards herbal and natural remedies as well as alternative medicine such as acupuncture. Many of these treatments have been used for centuries and, because they do not use mass-produced chemicals, some people feel they are less likely to have dangerous side effects.

Source C: A patient undergoing acupuncture

FASCINATING FACT

Scientific trials have suggested that many of the plants and herbs used in medicine in the past are effective. For example, the herb feverfew can help to prevent headaches, the pain-killer morphine comes from poppies, aspirin comes from willow bark and St John's Wort has been found to be effective against depression.

ResultsPlus
Build better answers

Why did so many developments in medicine happen in the late 20th century? (12 marks)

■ **Basic, Level 1 (1–4 marks)**
Answer makes general comments about developments in medicine in the late 20th century.

● **Good, Level 2 (5–8 marks)**
Answer offers one reason, such as scientific progress, and describes why developments in science led to developments in medicine, using examples.

▲ **Excellent, Level 3 (9–12 marks)**
Answer offers a range of factors, such as advances in science, technology and an increase in funding, and explains how each has contributed to the advances in medicine with precise examples. To get the highest possible mark, the answer would show how these factors combined to accelerate the pace of change – scientific developments happened quicker because better technology was available and because the work received funding.

Activities

1 Draw a timeline to show the major developments in medicine from 1900 to the present day.

2 On your timeline, colour code: a) developments that helped to treat illness and b) developments that helped to prevent illness. Use a dotted line to show any developments that are directly connected to each other.

3 How did war help the development of blood transfusions and penicillin?

4 Why does religion seem to have so much less impact on medicine in the modern period than the medieval period?

5 Does the increasing use of alternative medicine reflect continuity with the past, or a reaction against the role of science in medicine?

6 Draw an ideas map showing the links between the roles of war, government, science and technology, and key individuals' attitudes and beliefs in the modern period.

Summary

The period from 1900 to the present has been a time of many changes, but these changes have happened at different speeds and have not always led to progress.

3.11 The work of the historian: researching a controversy

Learning outcome

By the end of this topic you should be able to:

- understand the way a historian evaluates sources when researching a controversy

There are often controversies in history where the evidence offers different views and opinions. This investigation will consider the case of DNA, which you have already studied on pages 50–51. You are asked to consider whether Rosalind Franklin should receive more recognition for her role in its discovery.

ResultsPlus
Watch out!

The most common misunderstanding from students if sources contradict each other is either:

- to assume that one source is completely wrong and the other is completely right, or
- to try to find a compromise, where both sources are 'half right'.

The key, as always, is to evaluate each source and think about whether the author:

- might be mistaken
- has a reason to be deliberately misleading
- can offer proof to show that their version is correct.

Rosalind Franklin

Rosalind Franklin

- Born 1920.
- Studied chemistry at Cambridge University.
- In 1951 accepted a position at King's College London, working on the new technique of X-ray crystallography and leading a team studying DNA.
- Relations with Wilkins were difficult because he was already working on this topic and expected her to join his team.
- Took first photograph of DNA.

Crick and Watson, with their model of the structure of DNA

Francis Crick

- Born 1916 in England.
- Trained as a physicist.
- Shared office with James Watson from 1951.
- Began to research molecular biology and genetics.

James Watson

- Born in 1928 in America.
- Moved to Cambridge University 1951.
- Researched DNA.

Source A: Rosalind Franklin's X-ray photo of DNA.

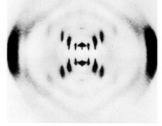

Maurice Wilkins – awarded the Nobel Prize along with Crick and Watson

Maurice Wilkins

- Born 1916, New Zealand.
- Moved to England when six years old.
- Worked at King's College, London.
- Expert in X-ray photography.
- Friends with Watson.

Stages in the discovery of DNA

1 Crick and Watson teamed up to try to build a model of DNA.

2 They made use of other specialisms and were very interested to hear of Wilkins' and Franklin's work.

3 Franklin looked at their model of DNA and pointed out something in their work that her photographs showed was a mistake.

4 Wilkins passed on further details of Franklin's work to Crick and Watson, and when Watson visited Wilkins in London, Wilkins showed him Franklin's most recent (and clearest) photograph.

5 Crick and Watson changed some details of their model to fit the evidence from her photograph and five weeks later their model was complete.

6 Franklin wrote up her findings and published them at almost the same time as Crick and Watson.

The Nobel Prize in 1962 was shared between Crick, Watson and Wilkins – but not Franklin because the Nobel Prize is not awarded posthumously and she had died four years earlier. This means that she tends not to receive the same recognition as the others.

Cases such as these can be approached in a number of ways.

- The historian may want to assess the role played by each person – for example, would Crick and Watson have discovered the structure of DNA without Franklin's photograph?
- The investigation may focus on how the discovery was seen at the time – why did Crick and Watson get the credit for the discovery of DNA's structure?

So how does the historian research a controversy? Just as with any other enquiry, the historian must look at all the available sources and evaluate them carefully in order to establish the facts without being influenced by other people's opinions (see pages 130–131).

Evidence about the role of Franklin in the discovery of the structure of DNA

Source B: From the outline of a BBC TV programme about Franklin.

Today, nearly all scientists agree that the hard evidence used to support Crick, Watson and Wilkins' theory about DNA was based on the work of Rosalind Franklin, a brilliant molecular biologist and crystallographer.

Source C: A comment from an article by Crick in 1974.

Rosalind Franklin was only two steps away from the solution but she was about to give up working on DNA. However, I don't think the discovery would have been delayed very much because Wilkins was going to work full time on the problem.

Source D: From a speech to scientists by Watson in 1999.

The truth is we should have worked out the structure of DNA at the end of 1951. We had enough information but we wouldn't have been sure that we were right without Rosalind's X-ray work.

Franklin was not part of Crick and Watson's team but her photograph was helpful in suggesting the shape of the DNA double helix. However it is not clear whether it was a crucial breakthrough – Pauling in America was also researching the structure of DNA and seemed close to a solution even without Franklin's photographs.

Activities

1 What evidence contemporary to their work might be available that could show the contribution made by each of the four individuals, Crick, Watson, Wilkins and Franklin, to the discovery of the structure of DNA?

2 How do you think historians should treat evidence from these people if it comes from a later time, for example, Watson's comment about Rosalind Franklin in a speech in 1999, shown in Source D above?

Medicine and treatment c1350 to present day: summary

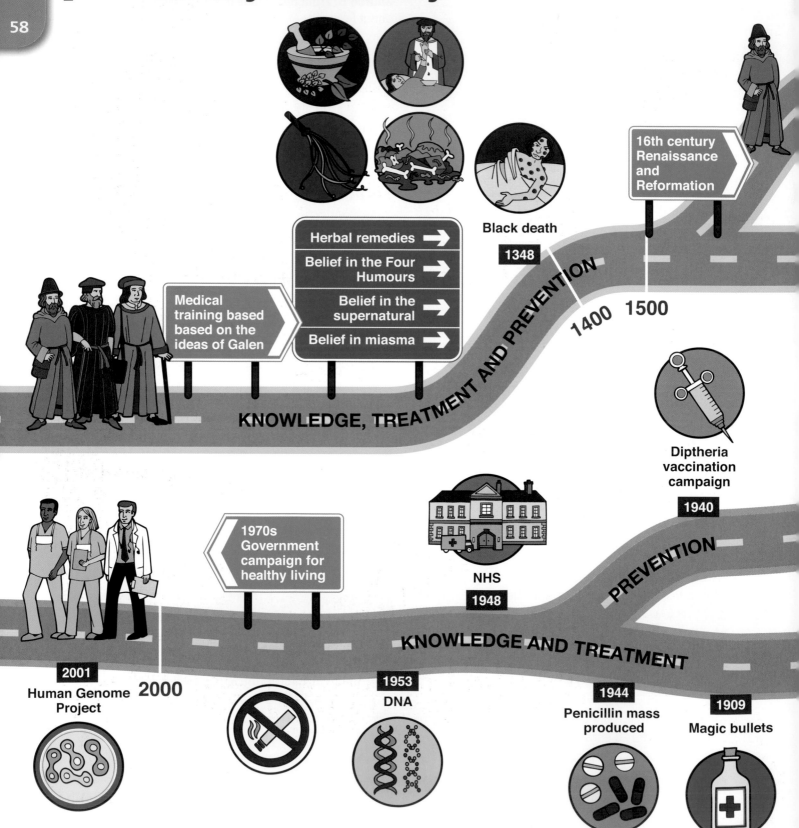

Herbal remedies →

Belief in the Four Humours →

Belief in the supernatural →

Belief in miasma →

Medical training based based on the ideas of Galen

Black death
1348

16th century Renaissance and Reformation

KNOWLEDGE, TREATMENT AND PREVENTION

1400 1500

Diptheria vaccination campaign
1940

1970s Government campaign for healthy living

NHS
1948

PREVENTION

KNOWLEDGE AND TREATMENT

2001
Human Genome Project 2000

1953
DNA

1944
Penicillin mass produced

1909
Magic bullets

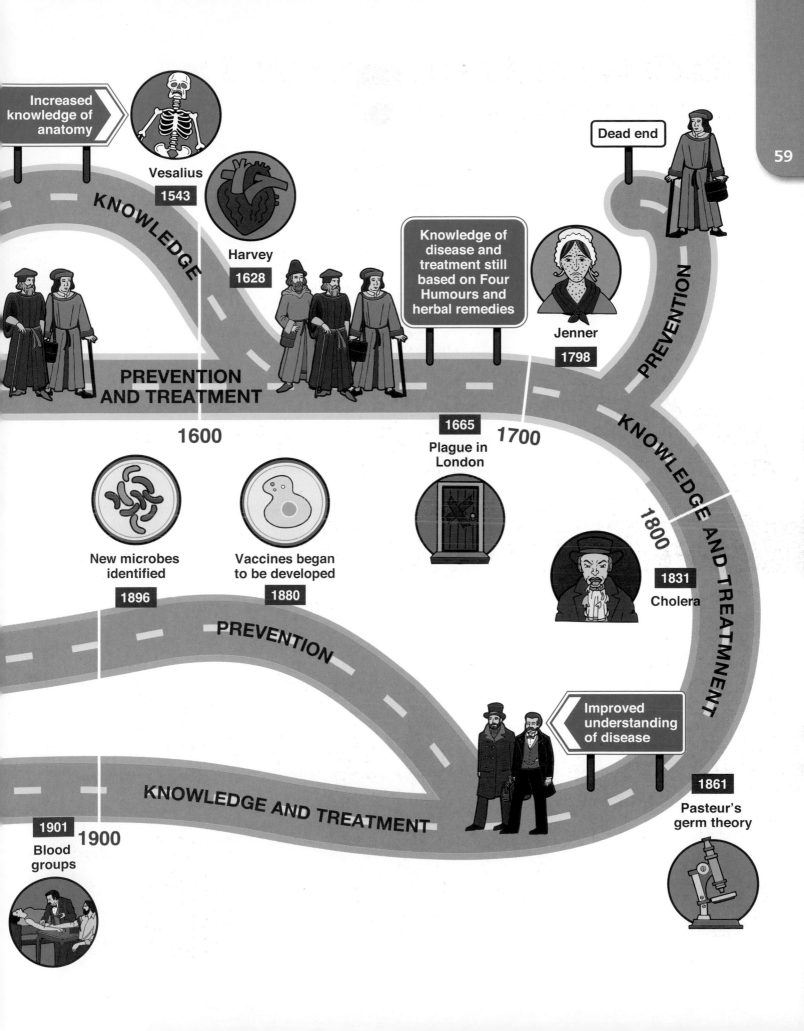

Increased knowledge of anatomy

Vesalius
1543

Harvey
1628

KNOWLEDGE

PREVENTION AND TREATMENT

Knowledge of disease and treatment still based on Four Humours and herbal remedies

Dead end

Jenner
1798

PREVENTION

1665
Plague in London

1700

KNOWLEDGE AND TREATMENT

New microbes identified
1896

Vaccines began to be developed
1880

PREVENTION

1831
Cholera

1800

Improved understanding of disease

KNOWLEDGE AND TREATMENT

1861
Pasteur's germ theory

1901
Blood groups

1900

KnowZone
Medicine and treatment

Introduction

For the Core part of the Unit 1 Medicine exam you have to answer three questions. The first question will always ask you what you can learn about an aspect of medicine from two sources. The two sources will normally be from two different periods and you will be expected to talk about change or continuity. The second question will give you a choice between two options and you then have a choice in answering either question 3 or 4.

As there is only a limited choice of questions in the exam so you need to make sure you have good knowledge of all the topics in the specification and that you are prepared for the different types of questions that are asked.

For the exam you can be asked to show examples of change or continuity in the developments in medicine, to explain why change happened at a particular point, or to assess how important something was. Questions can focus on a single section of the core or can ask you to make comparisons across more than one section.

Checklist

The key themes throughout the whole of the core are:

● ideas about the cause of disease, for example ideas about the supernatural, the search for a natural explanation of illness, the move towards a scientific understanding of illness and of genetic conditions.

● approaches to the treatment and prevention of illness, for example treatment based on plants and herbs, religion, treatment based on the Four Humours, vaccination, antibiotics and the move towards gene therapy, as well as the development of hospitals and the NHS.

● the role of factors in the developments in medicine, for example showing how religion encouraged the care for the sick but not a search for a cure, showing how changes in scientific knowledge affected approaches to treatment, the increasing role of government in organising medical care.

Another key aspect of these themes is how much progress was occurring within medicine.

Revision activity

Go back through your notes and through the textbook and summarise the key points in a table like this:

Period	Ideas about the cause of disease	Approaches to treatment and prevention	Factors affecting developments	Amount of progress
1350–1500 Middle Ages	Four Humours Religion Miasma			
1500–1750 Renaissance		Bloodletting and purging Herbal remedies		
1750–1900 Industrial revolution			Increase in scientific knowledge Improved technology Role of government	
1900–present Modern				Huge changes in both ideas about cause of disease and in treatment and prevention. Medicine is now able to deal effectively with many more types of illness but still cannot always treat genetic illness.

Student tips

When I was revising my teacher said I didn't need to learn many dates but it was important to know the order of events, so I wrote out lots of timelines. I also did ideas maps to show all the different factors that affected a change and I found it helpful to get a picture that showed a key aspect of medicine in a period and to annotate it.

Mini exam paper

1. Study Sources A and B.

   What can you learn from these sources about the changing methods of dealing with infectious disease? Explain your answer using these sources.   (4 marks)

You only need to use these sources to give a good answer

Notice the focus on changes – you'll need to explain the difference between the methods shown in the pictures

Source A: A drawing of a leper from the Middle Ages. He carries a bell to warn people to keep away.

Think about the question. How is the infectious disease of leprosy being dealt with?

Why are people warned to keep away?

Source B: Vaccination leaflet produced by the National Health Service in 1999. This tells people about a vaccination available to prevent the spread of meningitis.

Think about what the leaflet is trying to get people to do and why.

Use your knowledge of the historical context to think about who is involved providing in health care, and what they are able to do to prevent infection.

Mark scheme

Examiners have strict guidelines on how to award your marks in the exam. For the question we are looking at it would be like this:

1–2 marks – some simple statements and examples from the sources are used.

3–4 marks – some comments and an inference is made using both sources. This means you are doing more than describing the sources – you are developing an idea about changes between these two sources and are using the sources to support your explanation.

Now you are going to look at two sample answers below and compare them to the mark scheme above. What mark would you give each one and why? There are some clues to help you think about what mark you think each is worth

Answer A

In Source A you can see a leper and he is carrying a bell to tell people to keep away from him. In Source B the leaflet is telling people to get vaccinations. Vaccinations stop people from catching diseases. When Jenner first came up with his work many doctors were against it, but later on the government supported the use of vaccinations.

Answer B

You can learn from sources A and B that methods of dealing with infectious diseases have changed a lot from the Middle Ages. In source A they only know how to avoid catching the disease by keeping people away from infectious people, but they did not understand how diseases spread. In source B we can see that the government is playing a role in preventing the spread of disease by encouraging people to have vaccinations. So the methods used in B are based on better understanding of disease and a more effective action to control it but we can also see that the government is involved and the method is much more organised.

Questions 2, 3 and 4

There are various types of question which may come up for questions 2, 3 and 4. The examples below show some of these. On the next spread, we are going to have a look at some answers that students have given for two of these questions and see what the examiner has to say about them.

Questions which focus on continuity:
- Why did Galen's teachings on the Four Humours continue to be so important in the treatment of illness until the 18th century?
- Why did Jenner's discovery of vaccination have so little impact on the treatment of other infectious diseases in the 19th century?

Questions which focus on change:
- What factors helped Harvey to make his discovery about the circulation of blood and the importance of the heart?
- Why was the discovery of DNA so important in improving our understanding of the causes of ill health?

Questions which focus on making a judgement:
- How far did the role of the Christian Church and religion hold back progress in medicine in the period 1350–1750?
- How far was the role of women in medicine changed by Elizabeth Garrett Anderson's success in qualifying as a doctor?

Is this answer doing more than describing the sources?

Is this relevant to the question asked?

Does this answer discuss changes?

Is any of this answer irrelevant to the question?

Results Plus

Maximise your marks

Why did Galen's teachings on the Four Humours continue to be so important in the treatment of illness until the 18th century? (9 marks)

Student answer	Examiner comments	Improved student answer
The Four Humours were black bile, yellow bile, blood and phlegm. People thought that if you were ill it was because your humours were unbalanced and they would try to restore the balance by blood letting or purging or by telling you to eat certain things.	This is describing the theory of Four Humours but it is not answering the question. This is wasting time and not gaining marks.	According to the theory of the Four Humours, illness was the result of an imbalance in a person's humours.
Galen was a doctor in Roman times who wrote a lot of medical texts. His ideas were still being used over one thousand years after his death.	This recognises that the question is about why Galen's ideas were still being used so long after his death but it has not yet offered any reasons.	The Roman doctor Galen developed a system of treatment based on his theory. He wrote many books recommending treatment including blood letting, purging, rest, changes in diet and exercise.
One reason why Galen's ideas were still being used is that throughout the Middle Ages and Renaissance periods, medical training was controlled by the Church. The Church approved of Galen's teachings because his idea that the body was a single unit fitted in with religious ideas about how God created man.	This directly answers the question but only one reason has been given.	One reason why Galen's ideas were still being used is that throughout the Middle Ages and Renaissance periods, medical training was controlled by the Church. The Church approved of Galen's teachings because his idea that the body was a single unit fitted in with religious ideas about how God created man.
		Another reason is that medical training did not include dissections and therefore not many people spotted that Galen had made some mistakes in his explanation of anatomy.
		However, even when Vesalius and Harvey proved that Galen had made mistakes in anatomy, this did not affect the theory of the Four Humours or ideas about the cause and treatment of disease.
		Therefore Galen's ideas continued to be the basis of medical training until Pasteur's germ theory offered an explanation for disease that could be proved and at this point, medical treatment and training changed.

Overall comment

Some students will not understand the focus of the question and will not score highly on this question; many students will be able to explain one reason why Galen's treatments continued to be used; a few students will realise they need to explain more than one reason.

How far was the role of women in medicine changed by Elizabeth Garrett Anderson's success in qualifying as a doctor? (12 marks)

Student answer	Examiner comments	Improved student answer
Elizabeth Garrett Anderson worked as a nurse at the Middlesex Hospital in the 1860s and attended lectures for medical students. When the students complained about her joining their lectures she studied by herself.	This answer tells the story, describing what Garrett Anderson did but not explaining how any of this information answers the question.	Many obstacles faced women who wanted to become doctors. For example, they could not attend university and they were thought to be too stupid to train as doctors and too sensitive to be able to do the work.
In 1865 Garrett Anderson passed her exams but she needed to be accepted by one of the three official bodies. The rules of two of them stated that they did not accept women so she applied to the Society of Apothecaries. When they refused to accept her, her father sued them in court and eventually they had to agree to register her as a doctor.	This is still telling the story; the focus needs to be on what changed as a result of Garrett Anderson's success.	In 1865 Garrett Anderson passed her exams but she needed to be accepted by one of the three official bodies. The rules of two of them stated that they did not accept women so she applied to the Society of Apothecaries. When they refused to accept her, her father sued them in court and eventually they had to agree to register her as a doctor. This was an important breakthrough because it meant that she could now be registered as a doctor.
After they accepted Elizabeth Garrett Anderson, the Society of Apothecaries changed its rules so that no other women would be accepted. She also had to go to Paris to take her final examinations to receive her degree because British universities would not award a medical degree to a woman.	This is an important point but it is not explained.	After they accepted Elizabeth Garrett Anderson, the Society of Apothecaries changed its rules so that no other women would be accepted. This meant that other women could not follow the same route to become doctors. She also had to go to Paris to take her final examinations to receive her degree because British universities would not award a medical degree to a woman, so the situation had not changed very much.
In 1876 an Act was passed which allowed women to qualify as doctors.	This ending is not related to the question.	In 1876 an Act was passed that allowed women to qualify as doctors. This was an important breakthrough, which did finally change the position of women in the medical profession but it is not clear whether this was due to Garrett Anderson or was just part of changes in the position of women in society generally. Her career was not a breakthrough because the situation was altered after her but she was important in showing that women wanted to become doctors and were capable of it.

Overall comment

This answer would receive a top Level 2 mark of 8 – there is excellent knowledge here. However, the answer could not receive a Level 3 mark because it does not answer the question. The same knowledge could have got full marks if there was a clearer focus on the question – Garrett Anderson did overcome all the obstacles which prevented women from becoming doctors but her actions did not create a breakthrough effect because the situation was changed to prevent anyone else qualifying in the same way. Her work as a doctor (and Florence Nightingale's work in nursing) may have helped to change attitudes towards women in medicine but the biggest breakthrough was when a new law allowed other women to become doctors too.

4.1 Medicine and public health from Roman Britain to c1350: introduction

66

This section focuses on the first Extension Study: Medicine and public health from Roman Britain to c1350. As you study this, you should recognise most of the key themes about the process of change in medicine and treatment and you should be aware of the way this leads into the core section of the examination specification. Those key themes are:

- ideas about the cause of disease
- approaches to the treatment and prevention of disease and illness
- the influence of changes in society on medicine and treatment.

Before…

- The Ancient Greeks had developed an explanation for ill health based on the idea that it was caused by an imbalance in a person's Four Humours. Treatment could be based on changes in diet, and on encouraging the patient to get both rest and exercise. However, treatment could also be based on the idea of letting out excess humour through bleeding or purging the patient.
- At the same time, many people continued to rely on prayers and charms to protect and cure them, or would use home-made remedies based on the use of plants.

After…

- In 1347 the Black Death arrived in Europe and approximately one third of the population died. The understanding of disease was very limited and treatment continued to be based on the ideas of Galen but there were discoveries in the 16th and 17th centuries that began to improve the understanding of the body.

Dissection: Cutting open a body to examine its internal structure

Public health: The standard of living conditions and general health of the people

Purging: Getting rid of bad or excess humours by making someone sick or by making them have diarrhoea

Society: The way a group of people links together in some common ways

Surgeon: Someone who deals with wounds or with treatment that involves cutting the body

Roman society and medicine and public health

When the Romans conquered Britain in 43 CE, they brought their ideas about medicine and public health with them. The Romans adopted many of their ideas about disease and illness from the Greeks and there were few developments by the Romans about theories of illness. However, there were major improvements in **public health**.

These features of Roman **society** combined to give Roman medicine a very practical emphasis – they were interested in what they could do to improve health and less interested in what caused illness in the first place.

c460 BCE – 370 BCE

Hippocrates

43 CE

Britain became part of the Roman Empire

129 CE – 216 CE

Galen

410 CE

Romans left Britain

597

Ethelbert, ruler of Kent, was converted to Christianity by St Augustine

664

Control of Pope in Rome extended over Christian Church in Britain

c930

Leechbook of Bald

1348

Black Death reached Britain

How did Roman society affect medicine and public health in Roman Britain?

- Because Rome was crowded they were aware of the problems caused by infectious diseases.

- They had skilled engineers who planned and built great aqueducts to bring clean water to the cities and sewers to remove human waste.

- Romans realised that hygiene was linked to health although they didn't understand why.

- The government organised large-scale projects and raised taxes to pay for them.

- Romans took on whatever attitudes and beliefs seemed to work, including ideas from all over the Empire.

- The importance of the army in controlling the empire meant an emphasis on keeping soldiers healthy and on treating wounds rather than developing new ideas about treating disease.

- Many Greek doctors came to live and work in the Roman Empire, bringing Greek ideas with them.

Medicine and public health after the Romans

After the Romans left Britain in 410 CE, there were huge changes. A number of local leaders took control, many towns and cities fell into decay and Britain was attacked by various invaders.

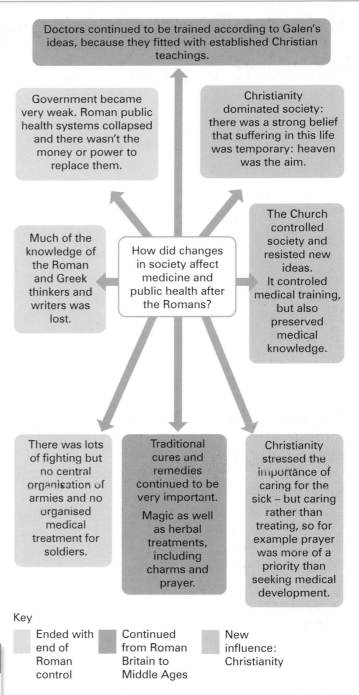

Activities

1 Why do you think public health was so important to the Romans?

2 Why do you think public health projects such as public baths or the provision of clean water needed to be organised by a central government?

3 Compare the two diagrams on these pages. What factors affecting medicine and public health would you say continued from Roman Britain into medieval Britain?

Summary

The fact that the Romans had an empire with strong government meant that their ideas about medicine and public health affected many people. However, the collapse of the Roman Empire meant that many of their advances were lost in Britain and there was little progress made in medical understanding and treatment for many years.

4.2 Medicine and treatment in Roman Britain

Learning outcomes

By the end of this topic you should be able to:

- understand ideas and treatments used in medicine in Roman Britain
- understand the importance of Galen
- understand that many Roman ideas were influenced by Greek ideas

The influence of Hippocrates on Roman medicine

The Greek doctor Hippocrates did not believe disease was sent by the gods. He believed illness had a physical, rational basis and could therefore be treated. His ideas were written down by his followers and had an influence on the way doctors were trained.

- Hippocrates said that a doctor should respect all life; if a doctor didn't know how to treat an illness, he should not try anything that could be harmful.

- Hippocrates developed the Theory of the Four Humours as an explanation for illness. Treatment was based on the idea of letting out excess humours to cure or prevent illness.

- Hippocrates developed the approach that became known as Clinical Observation, saying the doctor should:
  - study the patient's symptoms (breathing, heartbeat, temperature, and urine) and ask about how the illness had changed;
  - make notes and use knowledge of similar cases to predict what was likely to happen next;
  - once the predictions were shown to be accurate, correctly diagnose the illness and treat it – preferably through diet, exercise or rest.

The influence of Galen on Roman medicine

As you have seen on pages 6–7, Galen was a Greek doctor who worked in Rome in the 2nd century CE. This picture – done at a later time – shows a famous experiment by Galen where he cut certain nerves in a pig's spinal cord to prove that movement and the voice were controlled by the brain.

Source A: The dissection of a pig by Galen.

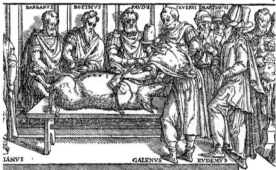

- Galen developed the ideas put forward by Hippocrates and suggested a new way of balancing the humours in the body through his Theory of Opposites.

- Galen had experience as a **surgeon** treating gladiators.

- Galen carried out **dissections**, although these were mainly on animals.

- Galen produced a number of books that were studied for the next thousand years.

Roman ideas about disease

The Romans had several explanations for the causes of disease:

- that there was a supernatural reason, for example that disease was sent by the gods or was a curse
- that it was caused by bad air from swamps or places where there were bad smells
- that it was caused by an imbalance of a person's humours.

There were very few doctors in Roman Britain and most illnesses were treated within the home by the father of the family, using remedies passed down by his father. These remedies used herbs and plants (such as a saffron salve for sore eyes) but also included ideas such as using oil and newly cut wool to relieve aches and inflammations. Many of these treatments were used throughout the Roman Empire and were described by the Roman writer Dioscorides in the 2nd century CE, when he published a book with detailed information on the use of plants and herbs as drugs. Other treatments might consist of bloodletting or **purging**, but often the Romans would mix these practical remedies with prayers and offerings made to Salus, the god of health.

FASCINATING FACT

Some people thought cabbage was so good for health that they recommended using the urine of someone who had lived on a cabbage diet to wash children to make their muscles strong.

Some of the medical ideas of the Celts already living in Britain were replaced by Roman ideas, but others were incorporated into Roman medicine; for example, the religious group called Druids made great use of herbs and plants, and the Romans continued this. Another example of the Romans' incorporating Celtic ideas is their name for the city that we call Bath; this was Aquae Sulis – which means 'the waters of Sulis' (Sulis was a Celtic goddess).

Roman Army hospitals were often well equipped and provided excellent training for both surgeons and physicians. However, there were few hospitals open to the public so this treatment and training would have had very little impact on the lives of ordinary people.

ResultsPlus
Build better answers

What developments in medicine were made by Galen? (9 marks)

■ **Basic, Level 1 (1–3 marks)**
Answer describes some of Galen's work and theories.

● **Good, Level 2 (4–6 marks)**
Answer describes and explains Galen's work in detail.

▲ **Excellent, Level 3 (7–9 marks)**
Answer defines developments Galen made in medicine by showing how things changed as a result of his work.

Activities

1 Look back at pages 6–7 and use the information here to explain how much Galen developed Hippocrates' ideas about the cause and treatment of illness.

2 Explain why treatment for illness was often a mixture of practical aspects, such as herbal remedies or bloodletting, and superstitious aspects, such as carrying charms or making offerings to the gods.

3 How much did the ideas of Galen contribute towards progress in medicine in the Roman period?

Summary

Many ideas in Roman medicine were based on Greek theories, especially the idea of the Four Humours. There were some developments, such as Galen's system of treatment known as the Theory of Opposites, but the Romans' main achievements were in public health, as you will see on the next page.

4.3 Public health in Roman Britain

Learning outcomes

By the end of this topic you should be able to:

- understand the key features of Roman public health
- understand the link between public health and medicine
- understand the significance of Roman public health measures

The Romans placed little emphasis on medical knowledge but they did notice that disease seemed to increase if you lived near marshes and swamps. This led them to suggest that buildings and cities should be sited in healthy places, away from swamps, because bad air (which they called malaria) caused disease.

They also recognised that there was a link between hygiene and disease, and although they could not explain what the link was, they stressed the need to provide access to clean water and to remove sewage. These features of the Roman way of life gradually spread throughout the Roman Empire, including Britain.

FASCINATING FACT

Archaeologists have discovered that Roman Britons disinfected their toilet sponges in vinegar.

Public baths in Bath

The Roman Baths in the city of Bath are some of the best preserved Roman remains in Britain.

The baths themselves were part of a whole complex of facilities. Admission was not free but it was cheap enough for most people to attend.

Source A: The links between Roman society and Roman public health

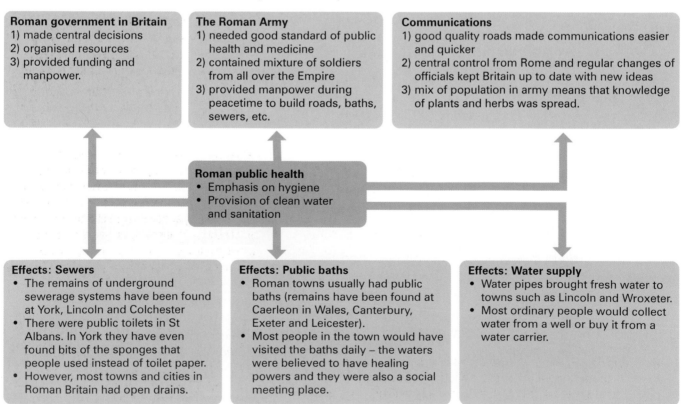

Roman government in Britain
1) made central decisions
2) organised resources
3) provided funding and manpower.

The Roman Army
1) needed good standard of public health and medicine
2) contained mixture of soldiers from all over the Empire
3) provided manpower during peacetime to build roads, baths, sewers, etc.

Communications
1) good quality roads made communications easier and quicker
2) central control from Rome and regular changes of officials kept Britain up to date with new ideas
3) mix of population in army means that knowledge of plants and herbs was spread.

Roman public health
- Emphasis on hygiene
- Provision of clean water and sanitation

Effects: Sewers
- The remains of underground sewerage systems have been found at York, Lincoln and Colchester
- There were public toilets in St Albans. In York they have even found bits of the sponges that people used instead of toilet paper.
- However, most towns and cities in Roman Britain had open drains.

Effects: Public baths
- Roman towns usually had public baths (remains have been found at Caerleon in Wales, Canterbury, Exeter and Leicester).
- Most people in the town would have visited the baths daily – the waters were believed to have healing powers and they were also a social meeting place.

Effects: Water supply
- Water pipes brought fresh water to towns such as Lincoln and Wroxeter.
- Most ordinary people would collect water from a well or buy it from a water carrier.

Source B: This picture shows the main bathing area as it looks today, but in the Roman period a visit to the baths had a hygienic and a social purpose.

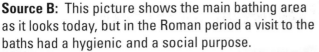

1 Before going into the baths both men and women would have done some exercise in the exercise hall: activities such as wrestling or ball games for men, games or weights for women. We know today about the health benefits of exercise; the Romans were also big fans of fitness.

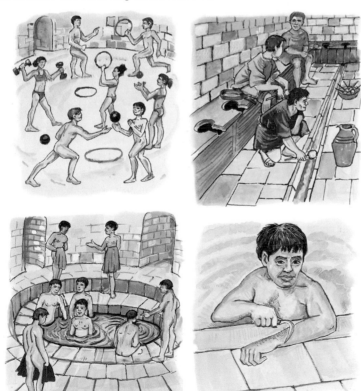

4 After steaming themselves in warm and hot water or saunas, Roman bathers would finish with a dip in a cold pool: the frigidarium. They would have left the baths a lot cleaner and more relaxed than when they arrived!

Activities

1 Design a brochure to explain the benefits of fresh water, sewers and public baths to the uncivilised people of Roman Britain. (Be careful to include only knowledge available at the time, so do not include references to germs.)

2 Use the diagram to explain the interaction between the army, the government and improvement in communications throughout the Empire as factors that provided a good standard of public health in Britain. Which factor do you think was most important?

3 'The main contribution the Romans made to medical progress was in public health rather than in the understanding and treatment of disease.' How far do you agree with this statement?

2 Public toilets in the baths were much less private than we are used to, but waste was removed from the baths by a sewage system and users had fresh water to clean their hands with. They would also rinse the sponge they had used to wipe their bottoms.

3 Bathers next went into a series of warm rooms; these could be steamy and damp like a Turkish bath, or a dry heat like a sauna. Here people were massaged with oil and then the oil was scraped off with a scraper called a strigil. This was a very effective way of removing dirt from the body. Roman Britons did not know about germs, but being clean would have helped keep them healthy.

Summary

Public health was a major feature of Roman civilisation and many towns in Britain benefited from having public baths and an organised system of sanitation.

4.4 Medicine and treatment in the Middle Ages in Britain

The labels 'Middle Ages' and 'medieval' are used by historians to describe the period between the Ancient World and the modern period, although they are not very exact (they are also not so relevant when studying Islamic, African, American or Asian history).

Treatment in the Middle Ages – no big change?

With no one taking responsibility for maintaining the structures built by the Romans, the public health facilities in towns fell into ruins. Although this had some effect on health and hygiene, it did not affect ideas about disease, and so the withdrawal of the Romans had limited impact on the treatments being used in medicine. Apart from Galen's Theory of Opposites, the Romans had shown little interest in developing their understanding of disease and illness any further. They had taken a practical attitude, which had included using local herbs and praying to local gods, and this meant that there was not a big change in medicine when the Romans left Britain.

They worked out many of the cures they used through a process of trial and error. They remembered successful remedies and repeated them even though they did not understand why they worked. Honey was a common ingredient – but not just to make the medicine taste nice; it seemed to help sore throats and cuts. We now know that honey has antibiotic properties and therefore using it as a drink or an ointment would have helped to prevent infection. Onions, garlic, wine and lichen from trees were also used often and are also all antibiotics.

Most folk remedies were passed down by word of mouth, but knowledge of plants and healing was sometimes written down in leechbooks (leech means healer). The most famous one is known as the Leechbook of Bald (Bald was the person who owned the book). A book of remedies written in the 13th century by Rhiwallon of Myddfai in Wales, it was unusual because it gave specific quantities of ingredients and methods of preparation whereas most recipes just named the plants involved.

Religion and superstition

The Christian Church became increasingly important during the Middle Ages.

- It was an international organisation across all Europe – an important channel of communication.
- Most priests could read and write and senior churchmen were often included among the king's advisers.
- Learning was preserved in the libraries of monasteries and convents.

FASCINATING FACT

A cure for toothache was to mix equal amounts of ground acorn, henbane seeds and wax and form the mixture into a candle. The smoke was to be directed into the mouth and a black cloth held underneath the mouth. It was thought the worm that was causing the toothache would fall onto the cloth.

Source A: A photograph of York Minster.

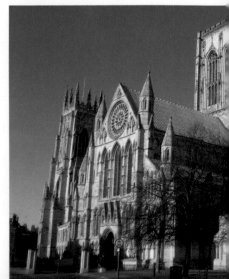

Treatments used throughout the Middle Ages often included a supernatural aspect as well as the administering of medicine. As Christians, people would say prayers and make offerings and might also go on pilgrimage to a holy shrine. However, many people would also carry a lucky charm or carry out a superstitious ritual such as rubbing snail juice on their eyes to cure blindness. Astrologers would also be consulted in order to choose the right time to carry out an operation.

Source B: A medieval diagram showing which zodiac signs and times of the year were linked to the different parts of the body.

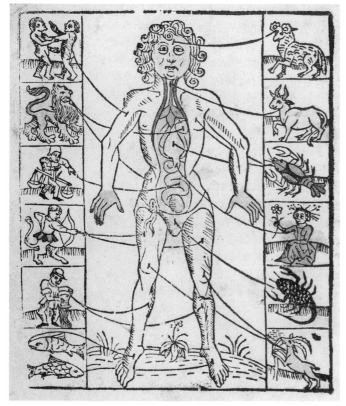

The influence of Galen

In the towns, richer people might consult a physician who was likely to use bloodletting or purging: treatments that were based on the Four Humours. Galen had been particularly keen on using bloodletting, both as a healing method and as a way to prevent illness. This was usually done by opening a vein and letting blood drip out into a bleeding bowl (these often had measuring lines around the inside to check how much blood had been lost) or by attaching leeches to the body (leeches suck blood and then detach themselves when they are full).

Activities

1   What examples can you find of medical ideas and treatment continuing from the Roman period into the Middle Ages?

2   What examples can you find of new aspects of medicine in the Middle Ages?

3   What factors affected the development of medicine from the Roman period to the Middle Ages?

4   Why was there such an emphasis on religion, superstition and tradition in medieval Britain?

5   How far does the evidence suggest that medicine did not progress in the Middle Ages?

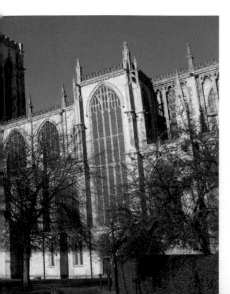

- Monasteries and convents often had an infirmarian, who cared for the sick.
- People believed very strongly in religion and accepted the Church's authority over their lives.
- People believed illness was a sign of sin, a punishment, or a test sent by God.

Summary

In the early Middle Ages there seemed to be little change in the sort of treatments being used for illness. The trained physician usually followed Galen's ideas, but there was little understanding of disease and therefore these treatments had little effect. Patients often combined treatment with prayers and charms.

4.5 Medical training from Roman Britain to c1350

Learning outcomes

By the end of this topic you should be able to:

- understand how medical training changed during the period from Roman Britain to c1350
- understand the factors affecting changes in medical training during this period
- evaluate the progress in medical training during this period

In the Roman period doctors were not highly respected. It could be seen that many of their treatments did not work and because many of the doctors in Rome were Greeks, the Romans felt that the foreign doctors were trying to take advantage of them. When Galen publicised his methods, many doctors hated him because he was arrogant and criticised their old methods – as well as being a foreigner!

- Alexandria in Egypt was the main centre of medical training because doctors there were allowed to dissect human bodies.
- The library at Alexandria held works from Greece, Egypt and India.
- There was no requirement for doctors to be formally trained.
- Most doctors 'trained' by reading books such as the Hippocratic Collection (the ideas of Hippocrates, collected and written down by his followers), or by working with someone who was already a successful doctor.
- There was no organisation to check that doctors were knowledgeable or to follow up complaints about bad doctors.
- Anyone who wanted to be a doctor could just set up in business.

At this time, medicine was thought to be closely linked to philosophy, and medical treatment was therefore part of a more holistic analysis of the person and their lifestyle. This explains why the idea of the Four Humours was so widely accepted and why treatment was often based on diet, exercise and changes to the patient's lifestyle, such as taking baths or getting more sleep. However, Roman medical ideas also gradually began to incorporate knowledge of plants and treatments from different countries throughout the Empire.

The effect of Roman medicine on Britain was fairly limited because Britain was on the edge of the Roman Empire and therefore few doctors would make the journey to Britain. However, each of the army legions sent here brought their own surgeons and, as some Romans settled here, their medical ideas began to spread. Although the Druid priests already in Britain had a good knowledge of plants and herbal remedies, this knowledge was passed on from person to person and was not written down. This meant that by the time the Romans left Britain, most doctors were following Roman medical ideas.

During the early Middle Ages there was little change in the training of doctors. Most of them continued to learn by reading books or by working with someone who was seen as a successful doctor.

The monasteries and convents had libraries that preserved many books. Some became centres of learning. Some of these grew into universities and offered training in the 'Arts', which included the study of rhetoric, geometry, astronomy and music. At first, medical training was undertaken in addition to a study of the Arts and took a total of ten years, so there were few doctors who trained in this way.

FASCINATING FACT

Books were so precious in the Middle Ages that they were often chained to the library shelves.

Source A: A 14th-century picture showing a physician treating a patient; the people behind the physician may be his apprentices.

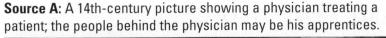

However, by the 12th century a separate course had developed and medical training was based on a set of texts that became known as the *Ars Medicinae* (Art of Medicine), including some works written by Muslim scholars. By the 13th century, most towns would not let a doctor set up a medical practice unless he could prove he had completed several years of study.

Education and training were controlled by the Church, and ideas and treatment were therefore slow to change. In particular, the Church approved of Galen and his ideas (look back at pages 6–7 to remind yourself why). Medical teaching was based on reinforcing Galen's ideas, and students were not encouraged to study anatomy or look for mistakes in Galen's teachings. The medical schools gradually became independent from the Church so that by the time of the Reformation in the 16th century the Church had lost control of medical training.

Activities

1 Why were there so few doctors in Roman Britain?

2 Why would many people in the Middle Ages have little confidence in a doctor?

3 Write a letter from a doctor who has just qualified to the head of a noble family in your area asking to be appointed to the household. Explain why you would be a good doctor.

4 Why was it significant that medical training eventually became independent from the Church?

Summary

The standard of knowledge and training of physicians did not change much between the Roman period and the early Middle Ages. In the 12th century life became more settled in Europe. As trade increased and the economy improved, towns grew much larger and learning increased. Universities and medical schools began to be set up and there was a greater emphasis on training for physicians. However, the level of knowledge and the sort of treatments used still did not change very much.

4.6 Public health in the Middle Ages

Learning outcomes

By the end of this topic you should be able to:

- understand the public health problems in the Middle Ages
- understand the role of government in public health provision during the Middle Ages
- understand the extent of progress or regress in public health during the Middle Ages

As towns grew bigger throughout the Middle Ages, the problems of hygiene became more important. People recognised there was a link to disease even if they could not explain what that link was, but it was difficult to keep towns clean.

Why was London so smelly?

London, as the largest city, had the biggest problems. In the 13th century lead pipes (paid for by the city authorities and from money given by individuals) were laid to provide water from the River Tyburn. However, there were leaks, the water was often contaminated and the supply was not enough for the city. Even when water was bought from a water seller, there was no guarantee that it would be clean. In fact, the quality of water was so poor that very few people actually drank it and most drank ale instead.

Meanwhile, animal and human excrement was common in the streets, rubbish was not removed, butchers slaughtered animals and left the remains in the street and rats were common. Laws were regularly passed, especially in times of disease, but they only had a limited effect – the systems were just too undeveloped to deal with the problem.

There were public toilets in London (and in places such as Leicester, Winchester, Hull, Scarborough, Southampton and Exeter) but we also know that people sometimes just relieved themselves in the street – in fact, one beggar boy died when he was run over by a carriage as he squatted in the street.

Source A: A picture of an English water seller drawn in 1338.

All this suggests that during the Middle Ages there was no progress in public health and that the standard of public health had regressed (gone backwards), especially in the towns and cities.

FASCINATING FACTS

In London in the 14th century it took approximately 100 barrels to remove the contents of a privy that was used by several households.

In 1326 Richard le Rakiere was drowned in a cesspit when the rotten wooden plank of his privy gave way.

Richard Whittington, who had been mayor of London, left money in his will to provide water outlets at various points in the city and a public latrine with 128 seats.

| 1281 The government attempted to stop pigs being allowed in London's street. | Government attempts to improve hygiene in towns and cities. | 1347 Sanitary Act tried to keep the streets cleaner. |

1388 a parliamentary statute complained that 'dung and filth... in ditches, rivers and other waters... so that the air there is grown greatly corrupt and infected and many intolerable diseases happen'.

On the other hand...

The situation was not completely bad. Rich people often had good standards of hygiene and would bathe in a wooden tub; many had a privy (toilet) built so that human waste was kept away from the living areas. Archaeologists have found that many houses belonging to merchants and bishops had lead pipes for a water supply, latrines and stone sewers.

Monks and nuns lived simple lives but the standard of hygiene in monasteries and convents was usually high. There would be fresh water piped to the building and the latrines were usually built over running water, which would take away the human waste.

Town councils recognised the importance of public health. Southampton improved its water supply in the 15th century after a merchant left a bequest for that purpose, and London, Exeter and Bristol had supplies of fresh water running through pipes or conduits to the city. There were also large baths, known as stewes, where people bathed together in large wooden tubs. Among the rich, this could be a very social occasion, with food and drink being shared, but the public stewes in towns were often denounced by the Church for leading to immoral behaviour.

Source B: Public bathing in the Middle Ages.

Activities

1. Make a list of all the public health issues connected with living in a town.

2. Town councils passed laws fairly regularly about keeping the streets clean, often repeating the same law a few years later. What does this suggest about the role of the local authorities in maintaining a good standard of public health?

3. Why do you think so few regulations were passed to improve public health in the countryside and villages?

4. Find examples of public health between the Roman period and the Middle Ages to show progress (improvements), stagnation (things staying the same) and regress (things getting worse).

Challenge

5. Research your nearest large town or city that has a Roman past. What public health did that city have in Roman times? What evidence is there of the local authorities trying to improve public health in the Middle Ages?

Summary

In Roman times, central and local government had a duty to provide a good standard of public health for the towns and used taxes and the army to do this. The situation in the Middle Ages was different and there was little organised provision of water or sanitation. The rich were not affected by this because they could pay for a better standard of living, and peasants were not too badly affected because the villages were not crowded. It was the poor people in towns who were the most badly affected.

4.7 Hospitals

Learning outcomes

By the end of this topic you should be able to:

- understand the types of hospitals that were established during the Middle Ages
- understand the role played by hospitals in medical treatment
- evaluate the significance of the role played by hospitals in medical treatment

As you saw on page 69, Roman hospitals were for the army; it was expected that other people who were sick would be cared for by their families. In the Middle Ages, hospitals were originally guest houses, and were usually part of a monastery or convent, offering hospitality to travellers. The first hospital in the sense that we use the term, of caring for the sick, was the Hotel Dieu, set up in Paris in the 7th century.

Care not cure

Over 1000 hospitals were established in England and Wales during the Middle Ages. Many of them were founded through charitable donations, for example St Bartholomew's in London in 1123. They were usually quite small (often they had 12 inmates in memory of Jesus' 12 disciples), although there were some large-scale hospitals, for example St Leonard's in York, could admit over 200 patients.

These hospitals were usually run by monks and nuns as part of their Christian duties because Jesus had said his followers should care for sick. The Benedictine monks made this a major part of their rules. There was also thought to be a strong link between religion and ill health because illness was often seen as a punishment for your sins. In addition, your outward body was often thought to reflect your character and soul, and therefore any disfigurement was interpreted as a sign of sin and evil. However, the monks and nuns aimed to care for the sick but not to cure them. Consequently, no doctor was appointed to St Bartholomew's, but several priests were, as it was felt that patients needed spiritual support more than medical treatment. In fact, people with infectious diseases or incurable conditions often would not be admitted.

This approach may seem strange to us but it is similar to the holistic approach used in many alternative medicines. Care for the soul, combined with the rest, warmth, food and care that patients received, could have meant that some patients did actually get better.

Source A: A picture of a convent in France showing the typical layout of a hospital. Notice that the patients are sharing beds although the covers and pillows are clean.

The food given to the patients at St Anthony's hospital, in London, included fresh salmon, turbot, shrimps, plaice, pork, capons, beef, geese, veal, rabbit, damsons, pears and apples. Although this was a wealthy hospital and the food was not typical, many hospitals grew a wide range of fresh fruit and vegetables.

The beds would also be positioned so that the patients could see the altar, religious statues and images in stained glass windows to help them focus on religion and be healed.

In the Great Hospital at Norwich, founded in 1249 by Bishop Walter de Suffield, women were welcome as nurses, but Bishop Suffield did not allow female patients and any women employed within the hospital had to be aged 50 or over, so that they would not distract the patients from their prayers.

Almshouses

Almshouses began to be set up in the 14th century to care for the 'deserving' poor and old. These people were expected to live according to quite strict rules about behaviour and prayer. Although they were cared for when they were unwell, the almshouse was not intended to be a hospital providing medical treatment.

Case study: the treatment of leprosy

Leper houses or lazars were places for lepers to live. Leprosy is a very unpleasant disease in which the nerve endings die and body extremities, such as fingers and toes, can decay and leave sufferers deformed. In the Middle Ages it was incurable. Throughout Europe lepers were expected to keep themselves apart from other people because they were infectious (they even had to carry a bell and ring it to warn people to move away).

Source B: A drawing of a leper in the medieval period. He is carrying a bell to warn people to keep away.

No treatment was available so the leper houses only aimed to provide care for the sufferers. Many were set up in the 12th and 13th centuries when there was an epidemic of leprosy but similar 'pest houses' were built later to isolate sufferers from the plague, which was also called the Great Mortality or the pestilence.

Activities

1 Imagine you are a wealthy merchant who wants to endow a new hospital as a way of earning God's favour. Explain which sort of hospital you would choose to found and why.

2 Why were the walls of most hospitals decorated with Christian religious scenes, especially the Last Judgement?

3 Why do you think people with infectious diseases and incurable conditions were not admitted to hospitals? What do you think happened to those people?

4 Draw a storyboard about a leper who is turned away from an almshouse and a hospital and is sent to the leper house. Include speech bubbles to explain why he is turned away until he gets to the leper house.

5 What does the treatment of lepers show about approaches to infectious diseases in the Middle Ages?

Summary

Religion was closely linked to medicine in the Middle Ages. Many hospitals were run by monks and nuns and provided care for the sick but they did not aim to provide medical treatment.

4.8 Factors affecting developments in medicine and public health

Learning outcomes

By the end of this topic you should be able to:

- understand that religion and government affected the development of medicine
- evaluate the ways in which religion and government affected the development of medicine

The role of religion

Emperor Constantine converted to Christianity in 313 CE, making it one of the official religions of the Roman Empire; after that, Christianity quickly became the main religion in Europe. As the Roman Empire collapsed, the Church was left as the only international organisation that could preserve and transmit knowledge.

As you have seen in the core sections, the role of the Church was an important one in controlling the training of physicians and in preserving the ideas of Galen. You have also seen how religion affected people's reactions to the plague and to the use of dissections.

Many religious saints came to be associated with specific conditions, so you would pray to St Anthony if you had a skin complaint, St Blaise if you had a sore throat or St James if you had rheumatism. It was also felt that the king, who was anointed with holy oil at his coronation, had religious powers. Scrofula was a form of tuberculosis (TB) that affected glands in the neck, and it was felt that if the king laid his hands on a sufferer, the disease could be cured – regular ceremonies were held, often around Easter time.

Religious institutions such as monasteries and convents often did a lot of caring work for the sick. The diagram in Source A shows how care for the sick was a central part of life at Fountains Abbey, in Yorkshire.

A painting of Fountains Abbey in Yorkshire.

Source A: A diagram of the floor plan of Fountains Abbey in Yorkshire.

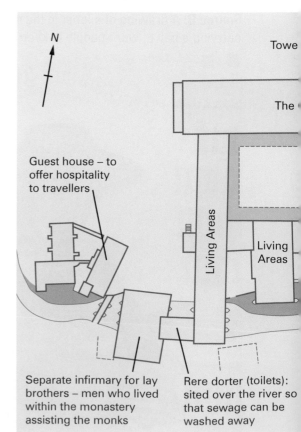

N

Towe

The

Guest house – to offer hospitality to travellers

Living Areas

Living Areas

Separate infirmary for lay brothers – men who lived within the monastery assisting the monks

Rere dorter (toilets): sited over the river so that sewage can be washed away

The role of government

After the end of the Roman Empire, the rulers in Britain were more concerned with protecting their people and trade from attack than with improving medicine. Even after the Norman Conquest in 1066, when the kings began to increase their control over the country, medicine was not a priority. This was partly because the Church controlled so many aspects of medicine and partly because there seemed to be very little that government could actually do.

In the Roman period, the government organised and funded the construction of a good system of public health but, after the Romans, when kings and central government did not make such work a priority, the standard of public health fell and local authorities faced many problems in trying to keep their towns clean.

People understood that cleanliness could help to prevent disease from spreading but there was no organised provision of public health. However, as towns grew and public health became more important, the local authorities began to be more active.

The role of war

War was responsible for the Romans settling in Britain. The control that the Romans imposed on much of Europe created prosperity for many and improved communications. In this way, it could be said that war had a positive effect on medicine in Britain, bringing knowledge from Europe. A negative effect of war was the fact that the Druids, who had a good knowledge of using plants in medicine, were suppressed when the Romans settled here.

However, when the Romans left Britain because of war in Europe, society became much more fragmented and public works were allowed to decay. War also disrupted society and trade. People were less likely to travel and exchange knowledge and there was less opportunity to build up centres of knowledge and training.

Activities

1 Use Source A to identify as many links between religion and medicine as possible.

2 Use this double page and the 1350–1750 section of the core material (pages 4–17) to draw a spider diagram summarising the ways in which religion affected developments in medicine.

3 Colour code your spider diagram to show (i) the positive aspects of religion's effects on medicine and (ii) ways in which religion held back possible progress in medicine.

4 Explain the problems that faced central government and local authorities when they tried to improve the standard of public health.

5 To what extent was the withdrawal of the Roman army a turning point in medicine in Britain?

Summary

Medicine in Britain has been affected by a range of factors, often acting in combination. These factors have had both positive and negative effects and their importance has varied at different times.

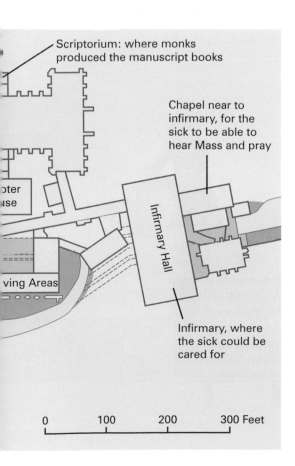

Scriptorium: where monks produced the manuscript books

Chapel near to infirmary, for the sick to be able to hear Mass and pray

Infirmary Hall

Infirmary, where the sick could be cared for

0   100   200   300 Feet

Medicine and public health from Roman Britain to c1350: summary

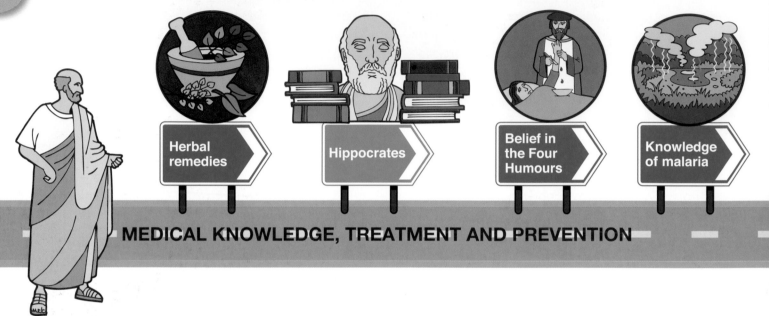

Herbal remedies

Hippocrates

Belief in the Four Humours

Knowledge of malaria

MEDICAL KNOWLEDGE, TREATMENT AND PREVENTION

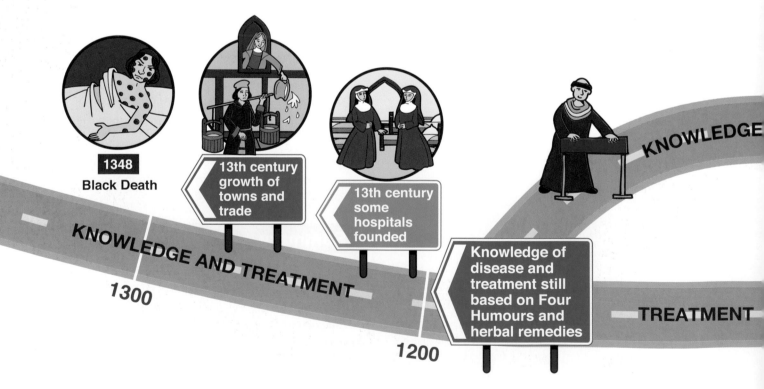

1348
Black Death

13th century growth of towns and trade

13th century some hospitals founded

Knowledge of disease and treatment still based on Four Humours and herbal remedies

KNOWLEDGE AND TREATMENT

1300

1200

KNOWLEDGE

TREATMENT

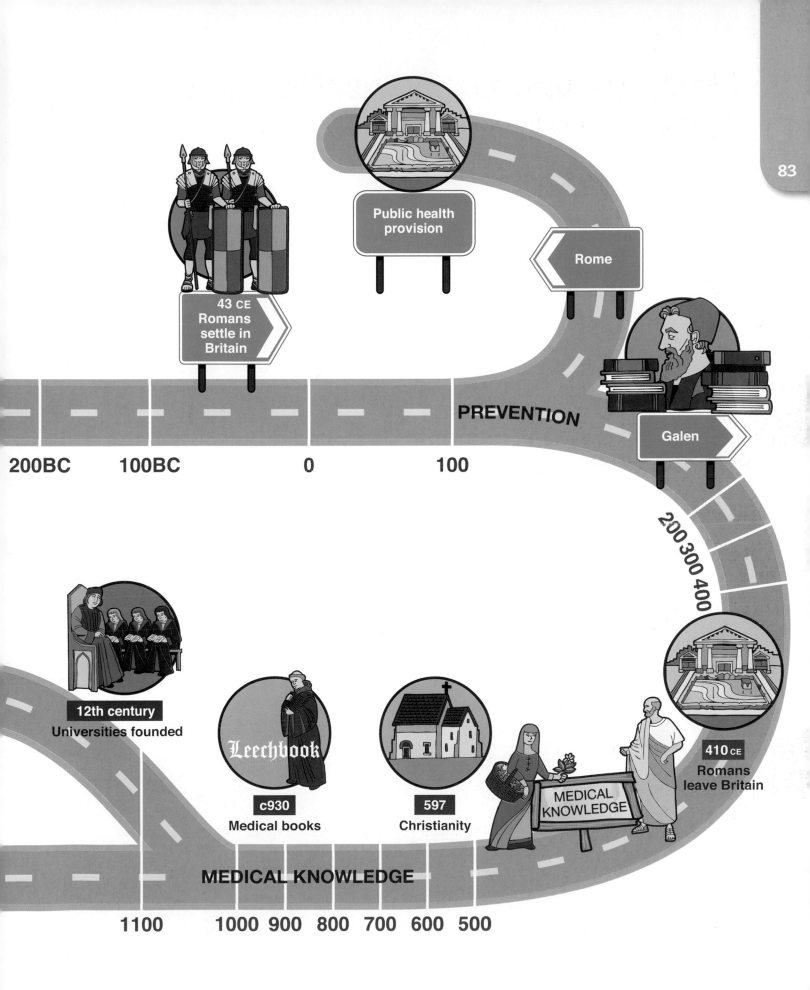

43 CE
Romans settle in Britain

Public health provision

Rome

PREVENTION

Galen

200BC   100BC   0   100

200 300 400

12th century
Universities founded

Leechbook

c930
Medical books

597
Christianity

MEDICAL KNOWLEDGE

410 CE
Romans leave Britain

MEDICAL KNOWLEDGE

1100   1000 900 800 700 600 500

KnowZone
Medicine and public health from Roman Britain to c1350

Introduction

This section extends the core topic by looking at the situation in Britain before 1350. The same themes are there, but the earlier period from Roman Britain and through the early Middle Ages is covered. You will be asked the same sort of questions as in the core and you may also be asked to link this section with the core when you talk about change and continuity.

There will only be one question (with two parts) set on this topic so you need to make sure you have covered the whole specification and you are prepared for the sort of question that is asked.

Part (a) is usually a straightforward question, asking about the key features of something. Part (b) will ask you for some evaluation or judgement. The (b) question will also have three bullet points like the ones here that help you to answer the question. By themselves, these bullet points will not be enough to answer the question but they should guide you towards the coverage that you need to answer this question well. You will also need to think of other examples and use them all to make a judgement. This sort of question does not usually have a 'right' answer – if you make a judgement and back your comments up with supporting evidence, you will get good marks.

Checklist

The key themes throughout this study are still:

- ideas about the cause of disease, but in this section the focus is on the early attempts to explain illness, for example the ideas of Galen and the Christian Church

- approaches to the treatment and prevention of illness, for example treatment based on religion, treatment based on the Four Humours, and medieval hospitals

- the role of factors in the developments in medicine, for example the role of religion in encouraging care for the sick but not the search for a cure, and the role of the government in Roman public health

- the extent of progress within medicine.

An additional element in this section is a study of public health throughout this period, in particular the standard of public health in Roman Britain and its decline in the medieval period.

Support activity

You may find it helpful to do a summary chart of the key events, as was suggested in the core section KnowZone (see pages 60–64), but an alternative approach would be to do a series of ideas maps similar to this one:

Public health

Galen's idea about treatment

The Romans in Britain

Ideas about treatment based on plants, etc.

Ideas about treatment based on religion, superstition, etc.

Exam-style questions

(a) What developments in medicine were made by Galen? (9 marks)

(b) How far was the progress made in medicine by the Romans continued in the Middle Ages? (16 marks)

- Romans built sewers in towns such as York and Bath
- The Romans left Britain c410 CE
- St Bartholomew's hospital in London was founded in 1123.

ResultsPlus
Maximise your marks

(b) How far was the progress made in medicine by the Romans continued in the Middle Ages? (16 marks)

Student answer	Examiner comment	Improved student answer
The Romans made a great deal of progress in medicine. They thought hygiene was important and they made great advances in public health. They used aqueducts and lead pipes to deliver clean water to towns. They also built sewers to take the waste away from the living areas in places such as York and Bath.	This answer makes some valid points about what the Romans did to improve hygiene, although it could have explained how clean water and the removal of waste was progress for medicine. It also just repeats one of the bullet points from the question without explaining why this was important.	The Romans made a great deal of progress in medicine. They thought hygiene was important and they made great advances in public health. They used aqueducts and lead pipes to deliver clean water to towns, which would improve people's hygiene and would also cut down on diseases spread by unclean water. They also built sewers to take the waste away from the living areas in places like York and Bath, which was important as some diseases are spread through infected sewage.
The Romans built public baths that everyone could use, and at the baths people would exercise and then have the sweat scraped off them, then go into the pool. There would be several pools, each one getting hotter, but at the end they would plunge into the cold pool.	This section of the answer provides a description of the public baths but does not link any of this information to the question.	The Romans built public baths that were very cheap so that everyone could use them. A higher standard of hygiene helped to reduce the spread of disease, even though the Romans did not know why. This all ended when the Romans left Britain c410 AD and these things fell into disuse, so the progress made by the Romans was not continued until the Middle Ages.
This all ended when the Romans left Britain c410 CE and these things fell into disuse, so the progress made by the Romans was not continued in the Middle Ages.	Again, a bullet point from the question is just repeated without being developed. There is an understanding that public health and hygiene are linked to medicine, but it is not explained. The answer would receive a Level 2 mark (between 5 and 8). Because it has very little extra knowledge and is focused on public health rather than medicine, it would receive a low mark within the level – 6 marks.	In other areas, the Roman standard of medicine continued. Traditional remedies were used and the works of Galen were the basis of medical training so that Roman ideas of treatment were not lost. However, some of these ideas were wrong, so it is not clear whether this aspect of medicine was actually progress.

5.1 Public health from c1350 to present day: introduction

This section focuses on the second Extension Study: Public health c1350 to the present day. 'Public health' means the overall standard of health of the population. This extension study looks at the development of public health from the mid-14th century to the present day and, in particular, considers the role of the government in bringing about improvements. As you study this, you should recognise most of the key themes about the process of change in medicine and treatment and you should be aware of the way this links to the core section of the examination specification. Those key themes are:

- problems of public health and their attempted solutions
- the impact of industrialisation and the reasons for the growth of government intervention
- the changing nature of state provision.

Before...

- Before the Black Death reached Britain in 1348, towns had been growing larger, with the result that hygiene and public health became an issue of concern, especially in London.

After...

- In the 21st century, the increasing cost of the **Welfare State** and the NHS is causing concern and some people have even been denied treatment because it is so expensive.
- There is an increasing emphasis on the need to adopt a healthy lifestyle and to take preventive action so that the risk of ill health is reduced.

Government action and public health

Diseases such as measles or smallpox are spread through contact with an infected person, while other diseases, including typhus and cholera, are spread through infected water, and some diseases, such as malaria, are carried by insects. Crowded

By-law: A law made by a town's local authority that affects only that town

Chamber pot: A 'potty' that was kept in a room or chamber, for people who needed the toilet and did not go to the outside privy or latrine

Laissez-faire: The idea that government should not interfere too much with industry and private business

Public health provision: Health provision for the whole community, such as the provision of fresh water, sewers and the availability of health care

Quarantine: The situation where someone who may have an infectious disease is isolated from other people to try to prevent the disease spreading; often the whole family was isolated

Welfare State: The coordination and provision by the government of all matters affecting the health of the people

Workhouse: An institution where people could go if they could not support themselves; they would be expected to work in return for their food and bed

living conditions, dirty water and the presence of refuse, human waste and animals such as rats all help to spread disease. Poor quality diet, hard physical work and cold or damp living conditions can also weaken the body's ability to resist infection.

The poster opposite was produced by the British government in the 1930s. It shows how far people's understanding of public health had progressed by the 1930s and also shows that the government accepted that it had a role in trying to encourage people to stay healthy.

1348
Black Death reached Britain

1665
The Great Plague in London

1842
Chadwick's report

1848
Public Health Act

1865
New sewer system for London completed

1875
Public Health Act

1911
National Insurance introduced

1948
The establishment of the NHS in Britain

2007
Smoking in public places banned in England and Wales

1350–1750	1750–1900	1900–present day
In this period the government's focus on preventing infectious disease started with some local authorities passing laws to stop people throwing waste into the streets.	By the 19th century a huge increase in the population had led to very cramped conditions and serious health problems. The pace of change started to increase in the late 19th century as the government began to pass laws to ensure the provision of fresh water supplies, the disposal of waste and improvements in hygiene.	By the early 20th century the government was starting to pass welfare reforms to improve the country's health and this led to the creation of the National Health Service (NHS) in 1948. In the second half of the 20th century the government became increasingly involved in health education so that people came to know more about the dangers of smoking, drugs and alcohol and the need for a healthy diet.

Summary

During the 19th century the government took on the responsibility of enforcing standards of sanitation, but in the 20th century the government's role in public health expanded to include the setting up of the NHS and an increasing emphasis on healthy living.

Activities

1 Suggest seven rules of health that the government in 1350 might have emphasised. Which rules do you think our current government would now suggest?

2 What would have the greatest effect in preventing the spread of infectious diseases:

   (a) improving the standard of housing to make them cleaner, warmer and less likely to have flies and rats;

   (b) providing access to a plentiful supply of clean water;

   (c) arranging for the removal of sewage from houses?

3 Why would it be helpful for local government to be involved in any attempt to improve the standard of public health in towns?

5.2 Public health 1350–1750: the problems

> ## Learning outcomes
> By the end of this topic you should be able to:
> - understand the increasing public health problems in towns
> - understand why it was difficult to deal with the public health problems in towns

As towns grew bigger during the medieval period, **public health provision** became a bigger problem too. Some attempts were made to deal with these problems:

- Some local authorities paid for piped water supplies and sewer systems.
- Some towns had public baths, called stewes, where people bathed together in large wooden tubs.
- Richer people might have their own latrines, which ran into a cesspit.
- Some towns had public latrines so people did not need to relieve themselves in the street.

You will find more details about the problems of public health in the Middle Ages on pages 76–77.

Medieval people were aware that there was a connection between dirt and disease, even if they couldn't explain it. The town councils passed **by-laws** ordering people to keep the streets clean and fined people who broke the rules. However, no one expected the local authorities to organise the removal of rubbish, and people had to pay for their cesspits to be emptied. In the same way, no one expected the king and central government to make laws about public health or to increase taxes, and therefore many of the improvements that happened were paid for by local individuals.

Case study: how could London get clean water?

In the 13th century, lead pipes were laid to bring water from the river Tyburn to London, and people would go to the pool of water at the end of the conduit (channel) to collect water. There were also water sellers who came through the streets, but the water was usually taken from a polluted river so most people drank ale rather than water.

Source A: The 'Little Conduit' at Cheapside. Water from the River Tyburn could be collected from the pool inside the building; this water was cleaner than water taken from the River Thames and was free to those who went to collect it.

Although London's council recognised the need for clean water, it could not decide what to do about it because it knew people would oppose any increases in their local taxes. Luckily two men were prepared to use their own money to improve the situation.

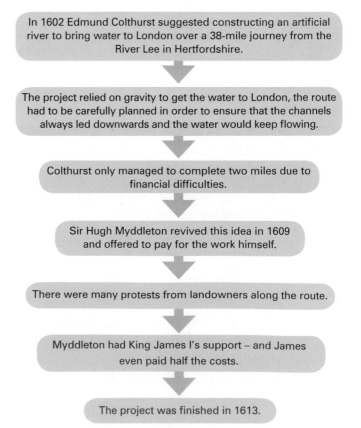

In 1602 Edmund Colthurst suggested constructing an artificial river to bring water to London over a 38-mile journey from the River Lee in Hertfordshire.

The project relied on gravity to get the water to London, the route had to be carefully planned in order to ensure that the channels always led downwards and the water would keep flowing.

Colthurst only managed to complete two miles due to financial difficulties.

Sir Hugh Myddleton revived this idea in 1609 and offered to pay for the work himself.

There were many protests from landowners along the route.

Myddleton had King James I's support – and James even paid half the costs.

The project was finished in 1613.

The project's completion meant that fresh water was available in parts of North-east London, but the supply could not keep up with the growing population of the city. Although some people continued to get their water from wells or water sellers, by 1750 most water was supplied by private companies, either piped to the house or available at standpipes on street corners, which were turned on at set times each day.

Sanitation: chamber pots and water closets

Although there were several attempts to improve access to water, there was little recognition of the need to improve sanitation. This had the effect of creating health risks, especially when sewage polluted the water. In medieval towns toilets were usually wooden seats above a cesspit, and people wiped themselves with leaves or moss. Several families might share one cesspit and ashes might be scattered over the sewage to keep the smell down, but it needed to be cleaned out regularly. These sorts of toilets were called earth closets.

Inside the house, most people used **chamber pots**, which were emptied into the drain in the middle of the street – or sometimes the contents were just thrown into the streets from an upstairs window.

Source B: Sanitation in the Middle Ages, from an old wood cut

The situation was not much better for the rich. The king had a 'close stool', which was a padded seat over a large bucket, and the most important job within Henry VIII's private rooms was the Groom of the Stool – the man in charge of the king's chamber pot! Meanwhile, at Hampton Court there was a 'great house of easement', which had 28 seats arranged on two levels. The waste emptied into brick-lined drains and then into the River Thames.

When Sir John Harrington invented a water closet (WC) in 1596, using water to flush away the sewage, Queen Elizabeth I liked the idea so much that she had a WC installed at Richmond Palace but many people ridiculed the idea and the WC did not develop properly until 200 years later.

FASCINATING FACT

Toilet paper was first used in Britain in 1857. It was sold by chemists – but it was not on display because people were embarrassed to see it, so it was kept under the counter. Toilet rolls were first sold in 1928. Soft paper was introduced in 1932 but was unpopular at first.

Activities

1 Write a letter to parliament in the 16th century trying to persuade them to pass a law to make all towns provide piped water, toilets and sewers.

2 What factors (i) helped and (ii) hindered the attempts to improve London's water supply?

3 To what extent did public health provision improve between 1350 and 1750?

Summary

In the medieval and Renaissance periods, public health became a problem for local authorities as towns grew bigger. There were some improvements in the provision of clean water but it was not organised or paid for by local or central authorities and there was little change in methods for dealing with sewage. At this time, the link between hygiene and health was not very clear.

5.3 Public health 1350–1850: government action

Learning outcomes

By the end of this topic you should be able to:

- understand the problems the authorities faced when dealing with public health issues
- understand the factors affecting the way authorities dealt with public health issues
- evaluate the role of central government and local authorities in dealing with public health issues.

In the Renaissance period, some cities and towns became very large; for example, London had a population of about 100,000 and in these conditions, infectious diseases were difficult to control. During an epidemic, local authorities often ordered a clean-up and might order barrels of tar to be burned in the streets to purify the air, while the king and central government might order a day of prayer. However, these measures would have little effect.

FASCINATING FACT

Henry VIII was particularly worried over an outbreak of 'the sweating sickness' at his court in 1528, which had a high death rate. He immediately left London and moved constantly to new residences, taking only a few people with him, including his best physician – his second best physician was sent to treat Anne Boleyn, who had caught the disease.

The role of local authorities in dealing with plague

An outbreak of the plague in London in 1665 killed about a quarter of the population. This put a lot of pressure on the town authorities and laws were passed to try to stop the plague spreading.

- They closed the theatres to prevent crowds gathering and banned large funerals.
- Dogs and cats were killed.
- Barrels of tar were burned in the streets.

Source A: There were several outbreaks of plague throughout the 16th and 17th centuries, but the most famous of these epidemics was in London in 1665.

- Carts came through the city daily to collect the dead bodies and bury them at night in large mass graves deep in the ground.
- If a case of plague was discovered, the whole household was boarded into the house for 28 days and a red cross was painted on the door together with the words 'Lord have mercy on us'.
- Days of fasting and prayers were ordered.

Most of these measures were ineffective and many people, including King Charles II, left the city. Even isolation and **quarantine** did not work because the disease was not spread by human contact but was carried by the fleas on the rats. Until Pasteur's work led to a better understanding of disease in the 19th century, neither doctors nor governments could deal effectively with infectious diseases such as the plague.

The role of government: making laws

The role of government is important in public health provision because only government have the power to pass laws to bring about changes. We can see evidence of this in the following two examples.

1 The problem of gin

There was public concern in the 18th century that cheap gin was having a bad effect on the poor. This is shown in the picture (below) by the artist Hogarth: the scene in Gin Lane suggests that strong alcohol has a bad effect on society. In 1750, the government passed laws that made gin more expensive. This was partly to try to improve the standard of health among the poor but also because the government was concerned about the effect on the economy if people were too drunk to work properly.

Source B: This picture titled 'Gin Lane' was painted in 1751 by William Hogarth. It warns of the dangers of gin.

2 Compulsory vaccination

When Jenner discovered a way of preventing people catching smallpox, the role of the government was crucial. Although the Jennerian society was set up to offer free vaccinations, many people still distrusted the idea of using cowpox to vaccinate against smallpox. The government made vaccination compulsory in 1852, but it was not strictly enforced until 1871 when an Act of Parliament forced local authorities to register everyone who was vaccinated – only then did the number of deaths from smallpox drop dramatically.

Activities

1 Why were public health issues so much more serious in towns than in villages in the countryside?

2 Make a list of the ways in which (i) the king and central government and (ii) local authorities dealt with infectious diseases such as the plague and smallpox. For each method explain how effective it would have been.

3 Why do you think central government did not raise taxes or pass new laws to improve the public health situation more often?

4 How far did compulsory vaccination and the tax on gin show the government taking on a new, preventive role in medicine?

Summary

As the population of towns grew and the living conditions became more crowded, disease spread easily. However, until Pasteur's germ theory, people did not understand how infectious diseases were spread and therefore the attempts of local authorities to deal with epidemics often failed. Central government rarely got involved in public health issues until the 19th century when there began to be the feeling that the government and parliament should take action in some cases.

5.4 Public health 1750–1900: cholera and Chadwick

Learning outcomes

By the end of this topic you should be able to:

- understand the factors affecting the work of Edwin Chadwick
- evaluate the significance of the work of Edwin Chadwick

During the Industrial revolution, in the late 18th century and early 19th centuries, the population of industrial towns grew rapidly. Housing for the workers in the factories was often of very poor quality and many families could only afford to live in a single room. In these conditions, disease spread rapidly, especially as there was poor sanitation and limited access to water.

Source A: An engraving of London in the early 19th century showing the crowded and unhygienic conditions in which most people lived.

FASCINATING FACT

In 1842 an investigation into housing in Bury, in Lancashire found that 63 families slept five or more people in one bed and 210 families slept four in a bed. Another investigation into housing in London found that in one ordinary courtyard, 120 people shared one toilet.

The growth in urban populations 1801–1851

Population	1801 (thousands)	1851 (thousands)
Glasgow	77	329
Liverpool	82	376
Birmingham	71	233
Manchester	70	303
Leeds	53	172
London	957	2,362

There was already a great deal of concern over the death rate from typhoid fever and tuberculosis, but in 1831 a new disease appeared – cholera. Thousands died within a few weeks and as there were other epidemics later, the local authorities came under pressure to take action.

Source B: A cartoon called 'A Court for King Cholera' showing that people at the time understood that cholera was likely to spread in dirty conditions.

A COURT FOR KING CHOLERA.

Chadwick's role in improving public health

Local authorities were expected to use taxes to make provision in **workhouses** for those who were too old, too weak or too ill to support themselves. Edwin Chadwick was secretary to the commission in overall charge of the workhouses. In 1842 Edwin Chadwick published the results of his survey of housing conditions in towns called *The Sanitary Conditions of the Labouring Population*. He suggested it would be cheaper if local taxes (rates) were used to improve housing and hygiene rather than paying for sick people to be supported in the workhouses.

Specific suggestions made by Chadwick were about improvements in providing access to clean water, and the removal of sewage and rubbish. However, Chadwick's suggestions were criticised by some when the report was published.

- At this time there was an attitude of **laissez-faire**, which was the belief that the government should not interfere in ordinary lives or business.
- The water companies objected to Chadwick's ideas because they thought changes might reduce their profits.
- Middle class people, who had to pay these local rates, did not see why their money should be taken to provide better living conditions for the poor who did not pay anything towards these improvements.

In 1842 Chadwick's ideas got a lot of attention, but little was actually done. Many people were angry at the idea that the government should insist on piped water and sewers - their complaints led to these protesters being nicknamed the 'Dirty Party'. However, another cholera epidemic in 1848 led the government to try out some of Chadwick's ideas.

Activities

1 If people recognised the link between hygiene and health, why did they not do more to improve the situation?

2 How did the following factors prevent Chadwick from being more effective: lack of scientific knowledge about disease; limited role of government in public health; and people's attitudes towards health and government action?

3 Chadwick did not properly understand the link between health and hygiene, and the reforms based on his ideas were all temporary – does that mean Chadwick was a failure?

Government action

The Public Health Act in 1848 set up a General Board of Health, with Chadwick as one of the three commissioners. It also allowed towns to:

- set up their own local Board of Health
- appoint a local medical officer
- organise the removal of rubbish
- build a sewer system.

But it did not force town councils to do this. Only one-third of towns set up a Board of Health and even fewer appointed a medical officer. Meanwhile the terms of the Act were only temporary so that in 1854 the three commissioners had to resign and the General Board of Health was abolished in 1858. Chadwick was not appointed to any other offical position.

ResultsPlus
Build better answers

What part did Edwin Chadwick play in bringing about changes in public health provision? Explain your answer. (9 marks)

Basic, Level 1 (1–3 marks)
Answer offers a simple description of something Chadwick did.

Good, Level 2 (4–6 marks)
Answer describes some of Chadwick's work and it includes specific information.

Excellent, Level 3 (7–9 marks)
Answer gives a detailed account of Chadwick's work and shows that he had a limited impact. The best answers will explore his work in the context of other developments.

Summary

The problems of overcrowding, poor housing conditions, and poor sanitation led to many deaths from disease. Epidemics of cholera killed thousands but Chadwick's report highlighted the issues and laid the basis for reform.

5.5 Public health 1850–1900: government action

Learning outcomes

By the end of this topic you should be able to:

- understand the action taken by local and central government to improve public health
- understand the factors affecting the work of the authorities in improving public health
- understand the significance of the work done by the authorities in improving public health

Mapping a connection – Dr John Snow's investigation

In 1854 there was another outbreak of cholera in London, and Dr John Snow used it to investigate his theory that cholera was spread through infected water. He marked on a map all the deaths in one area, and there was a clear concentration of deaths around the water pump on Broad Street. Snow had the handle of that pump removed so that water could not be collected and the number of deaths fell dramatically.

Source A: A section of John Snow's map showing deaths from cholera in 1854 in the Soho area of London.

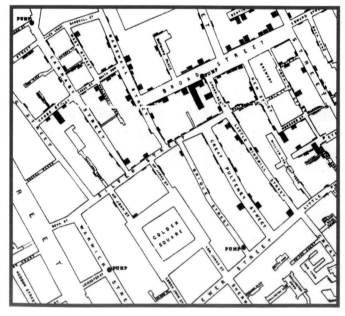

Source B: A cartoon about the Broad Street pump, called 'Death's Dispensary'.

Parliament slowly became convinced that it should take action to improve public health.

- Snow's work seemed to prove there was a link between water and cholera.
- Pasteur's germ theory showed how disease spread and why hygiene was important.
- Snow also showed that death rates varied according to the water sources used by different water companies.
- The government started collecting statistics on births, marriages and deaths; William Farr studied these and showed that the death rates were much higher in the towns and cities than in villages.

FASCINATING FACT
Queen Victoria was so excited about the new large sewer tunnels that she ordered a small railway line to be installed to transport people through the sewer. Gas lights and walkways were installed, with booths selling souvenirs.

The 'Great Stink' 1858

Plans were already being made for a new sewer system in London in 1858. However, the hot weather meant that the level of the River Thames was low and the smell of the exposed sewage along its banks was so great that parliament could not meet, even though sheets soaked in disinfectant were hung at the windows to cover up the smell. This 'Great Stink' persuaded the Metropolitan Board of Works to agree to the expensive ideas being put forward by Joseph Bazalgette. He was appointed to build a new sewer system in London, which took seven years to complete. By 1865, London had 1,300 miles of sewers.

Local councils take action

Another outbreak of cholera in 1866 least affected those towns where there had already been some improvements in public health. This reinforced the link between hygiene and health. When working-class men living in towns got the vote in 1867, this put even more pressure on the government and on local councils to take action. A good example of this is that in the 1870s, Joseph Chamberlain, the mayor of Birmingham, carried out several reforms, including the demolition of 40 acres of slums.

Act	Key terms
1866 Sanitary Act	All towns *had* to appoint inspectors to check water supplies and drainage.
1875 Artisans Dwelling Act	Local authorities were given the power to buy and demolish slum housing.
1875 Public Health Act	Towns had to appoint Health Inspectors and Sanitary Inspectors; local authorities were given powers to enforce regulations on water supplies and sanitation.
1878 Public Health Act	This consolidated existing laws.

By 1875 local councils were responsible for ensuring that:

- clean water was provided
- streets were paved
- rubbish was removed
- sewers were built
- the quality of housing was improved.

Local councils also became responsible for checking the quality of food in the shops to ensure that sand or chalk had not been mixed into flour, bread or sugar and that meat had not been dyed to make it look fresh.

Activities

1 Research: find out about the Great Stink of 1858 and the work of Joseph Bazalgette who designed and constructed a sewer system for London. Then write a newspaper article set in 1866 arguing either that this work has been a great advance in public health or a huge waste of money.

2 The role of government included central government, which made the laws, and that of local authorities, which organised and funded the changes. Which of these two aspects do you think was most responsible for the improvements in public health?

3 The reforms of 1875 went much further than the reforms of 1848. Why were they accepted when there had been so much opposition to earlier ideas?

Summary

In the second half of the 19th century there was greater acceptance of the need for action by central government and local authorities to improve public health. Change was rapid and far-reaching.

5.6 Public health 1900–1948: the foundation of the Welfare State

Source A: A slum in Whitechapel, London in the early 20th century; the poor standard of health of people living in such conditions put pressure on the government to take more action.

Access to health care

Despite the public health reforms of the late 19th century, the standard of living among the poor remained very low. Surveys showing how difficult it was for the poor to afford decent housing and food were carried out by Charles Booth (in the period 1891–1903) and Seebohm Rowntree (in 1888–1901). Then, when Britain was involved in the Boer War in South Africa in 1899–1902, a third of volunteers for the army had to be turned down because they were not medically fit (this figure rose to nearly 90 per cent in slum areas in northern industrial cities such as Manchester). This shocked many politicians and made them decide to take action.

The Liberal government that was elected in 1905 began to pass laws that they hoped would improve health among the poor. The diagram shows some of the early steps. The 1911 National Insurance Act was particularly important. Every worker earning less than £160 a year was expected to join the scheme, in which contributions by the worker, employer and government were made to a fund. Workers were then entitled to:

- free medical treatment and medicine
- sick pay for up to six months and support payment while unemployed for up to 15 weeks.

Source B: The beginnings of the Welfare State in the early 20th century.

Although the 19th-century idea of laissez-faire was now less common, there was some resistance to the government's increasing involvement in people's lives. Also, some people resisted these welfare reforms because of the cost. Although he eventually succeeded, there was a crisis in parliament when the Chancellor, Lloyd George, needed to raise taxes to pay for the National Insurance Act, which was passed in 1911.

In 1919, a Ministry of Health was set up and the government began to build sanatoria to care for people with TB, but there were still some problems.

- An epidemic of influenza in 1918–1919 showed that there were not enough free hospital places to cope with the sick.
- Women and children were not covered by the National Insurance scheme and so they often delayed getting treatment because they could not afford to pay for a doctor.

However, the average life expectancy by 1931 had risen to 58 for males and 62 for females, and the government was doing much more to help improve the health of the nation.

For example:

- secondary school pupils received medical inspections
- free milk for poor primary schoolchildren was introduced in 1934
- health clinics gave vaccinations and sold baby food cheaply
- many hospitals were brought under the control of local authorities.

There was also a range of private health insurance schemes that could provide treatment for women, children and those men not covered by the government scheme.

These developments must also be seen in the context of the events you have read about on pages 86–95: a better understanding of disease, the development of a range of vaccinations and the development of better treatment for disease. These changes meant that people's expectations of medicine increased and they were far more willing than previously to accept government interaction.

The effects of the Second World War

As you have seen in the core sections, the Second World War (1939–1945) had a major effect on people's awareness of the effects of poverty on health. People were shocked to find out that many children evacuated from towns were not used to running water or proper toilets and that they often had nits, lice or skin infections. This was an important factor in creating the desire for a higher standard of health after the war and the setting up of the National Health Service (NHS). However, the war also had an effect on people's diets. Food was rationed and fats

and sugar were in short supply, while people were encouraged to eat more vegetables, with the result that some people, especially among the poor, found their health was actually better than it had been in the 1930s.

Source C: Children in Bradford having a bath to get rid of lice and fleas. Poor children evacuated from cities in the war often needed to be treated for lice, fleas, nits and skin infections.

Activities

1. How far did public health improve during the early 20th century?

2. In what ways were the Liberal reforms of 1905–1911 a turning point in public health?

3. Research: find out how Lloyd George and the Liberals dealt with the opposition to the 'People's Budget', which was to raise money for the 1911 National Insurance Act.

4. What public health problems still existed by the start of the Second World War in 1939?

5. Which factor had the most effect on public health in the early 20th century – war or the role of government? Explain your answer.

Summary

During the early 20th century, central government intervened in a wide range of public health issues although local authorities were often responsible for actually carrying out many of the measures.

5.7 Public health 1948 to present day: prevention and education

Learning outcomes

By the end of this topic you should be able to:

- understand the actions taken by government after 1948 to improve public health
- understand how the role of government in public health changed after 1948
- evaluate the extent and nature of the change in the government role in public health after 1948

The NHS

As you have seen on pages 96–97, the creation of the NHS in 1948 was a landmark event in public health in Britain. The government had gradually been taking more responsibility for the provision of sanitation, etc., and then had made attempts to improve the standard of living and access to health care. Now a national system that offered comprehensive care 'from cradle to grave' was put in place and funded by the government. However, deeper understanding of both disease and the effects of people's lifestyle on health has led to a wider role for the government, emphasising prevention of illness.

Public health – preventive developments

The preventive aspect of public health has expanded since the Second World War in many ways. For example:

- developments in vaccinations, such as Jonas Salk's polio vaccine in 1952, and the introduction of a vaccine in 2008 against cervical cancer
- government campaigns and laws on health issues such as smoking
- government promotion of healthy diets
- better disposal of rubbish and treatment of sewage

- laws to reduce air and water pollution, for example the 1956 Clean Air Act, which dealt with the problem of smog (a mixture of fog and smoke from coal fires, industry and car fumes)
- laws to improve people's working conditions, for example health and safety regulations about asbestos in the workplace
- provision of environmental health officers to inspect restaurants, cafes and bars
- strict laws on food safety in 1990 after outbreaks of salmonella, *E. coli* poisoning, and BSE in cattle.

Health education

Smoking proved very popular in the mid-20th century when cigarettes became very cheap. However, in the mid-1960s it became clear that there were links between smoking and cancer, heart disease and many other health issues.

- In 1962 the Royal College of Physicians called for a ban on tobacco advertising.
- The government began taxing cigarettes heavily.
- Since 1971 packets of cigarettes have carried a health warning.
- In 2004 it was reported that over half a million admissions to hospital and 1 in 6 deaths were as a result of smoking.
- In 2005 a ban was placed on most forms of tobacco advertising.
- Smoking in public places was banned in 2006 in Scotland and in 2007 in England and Wales.

Source A: Government legislation means that every packet of cigarettes has to carry a very obvious health warning.

Similar government action has been taken over obesity in school children and there is concern about binge drinking of alcohol. In all these cases, communication has played an important role in the government campaign, with messages on the products, posters and television campaigns to raise awareness of the effects on people's health of their behaviour. When new health risks appear, the government has a key role in providing information to the public and support for sufferers. When HIV/AIDS was recognised as a significant risk to health in the 1980s, the government funded a national information campaign under the slogan: 'AIDS: don't die of ignorance'.

Source B: The chef Jamie Oliver led a campaign to encourage children to choose healthier options for school dinners, which influenced government action.

FASCINATING FACT

It is estimated that there are 60 million rats in Britain – and that a 24 per cent increase over the last few years is partly the result of fast food being thrown away on streets. Another reason for the increase is that water companies have not set as many traps for rats in their sewers as they used to. A female rat will live about 18 months and can have a litter every month – producing a potential 2,000 rats within a single year.

Public health and private companies

Private companies are increasingly involved in public health:

- some people use private health care instead of the NHS
- the responsibility for the provision of water has now been passed to private companies but the fact that many of the pipes are over 100 years old and need repairs or to be replaced causes problems for the water companies, who are reluctant to carry out the repairs because of the cost.

Activities

1 What additional responsibilities in public health has the government taken on since the second half of the 20th century?

2 How far do you think the creation of the NHS was a turning point in the nature of government involvement in public health?

3 How far do you think the government should regulate health issues such as sex education or the availability of alcohol?

4 How far do you think that aspects of public health being controlled by private companies could lead to regress (a lowering of standards) in public health?

Summary

The creation of the NHS was extremely important for the improved access to health care in the mid-20th century. In the second half of the century, the government took on an increasingly active role in attempts to prevent ill health and in educating people to take more responsibility for their own health, but there has also been an increased involvement of private companies in public health.

5.8 Factors affecting public health c1350 to present day

Factor 1: technology

You have seen how important the role of government has been in improving public health, but the role of technology is also important. The pictures show the size of the sewers created by Bazalgette, the construction work needed to build the underground sewer system for London, and the complexity of the planning and engineering that went into the system.

Technology was also used in the 19th century to pump water into the towns and cities in great quantities. The vast pumping system in Source C was installed in 1868 in the north of England and could pump 3 million gallons of water a day. This would have been impossible to achieve before the technological developments of the Industrial Revolution.

Source A: A photograph of Bazalgette inspecting the construction of the London sewer system.

Source B: An illustration showing the planning and engineering work involved in the construction of London's underground sewer system.

Source C: A pumping station built during the Industrial revolution.

Technology has also meant that living conditions have improved, with heating, hot water and electric lighting.

Factor 2: the significance of key individuals

Another factor affecting improvements in public health has been the role of key individuals. However, it is important to place each person in the context of what else was happening at the time.

Source D: Health Minister Aneurin Bevan visiting one of the first patients being treated under the NHS system in 1948.

Chadwick drew attention to the poor living conditions in towns.

John Snow showed the link between cholera and water.

William Farr and Snow used statistics to analyse the problem.

Pasteur showed that disease was spread by microbes.

The Beveridge Report in 1942 suggested the government should improve public health.

⬇

The new Labour government elected in 1945 accepted these recommendations and began to plan the NHS.

⬇

Bevan was the Minister for Health.
Bevan faced great opposition from doctors who did not want to lose their income from private patients.

⬇

Bevan publicised his ideas and persuaded patients they should ask to be registered as NHS patients.

⬇

This put pressure on the doctors to join the NHS or lose their patients.

⬇

The NHS was launched in 1948.

⬇

However, the cost of the NHS was much greater than anticipated and prescription charges were introduced in 1951 – Bevan resigned, feeling that this was a betrayal of all he had worked for.

Activities

1 Draw a ideas map of the events in 19th-century public health, showing:
  a) key individuals
  b) changes in scientific knowledge and understanding
  c) government action.

2 Explain who you think made the greater contribution to improving public health – Chadwick in the 19th century or Bevan in the 20th century.

Challenge

3 Find out about public health provision now. How much of the local rates is spent on sanitation and the removal of rubbish? How is sewage dealt with? What is the cost of water rates in your area and what are the responsibilities of the water company?

Summary

The role of government is a key factor affecting public health as both central government and local authorities are responsible for regulations and public health provision. However, the standard of technology that became available in the 19th century was important in allowing many advances to be made. Key individuals were important in accelerating change or steering its direction.

Public health from c1350 to present day: summary

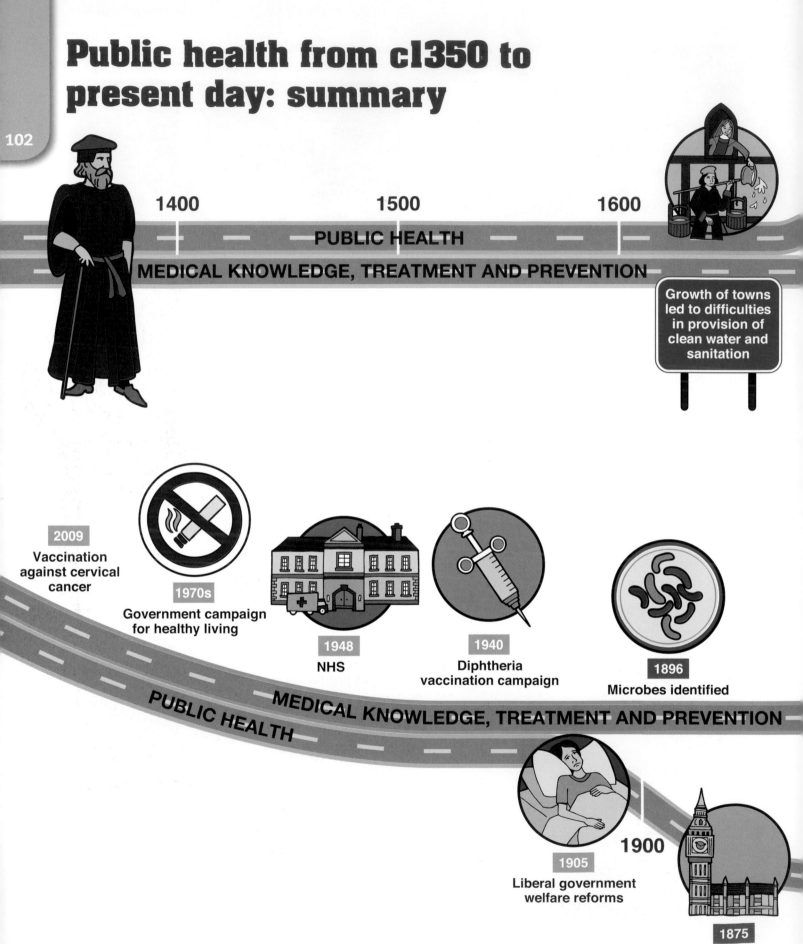

1400   1500   1600

PUBLIC HEALTH

MEDICAL KNOWLEDGE, TREATMENT AND PREVENTION

Growth of towns led to difficulties in provision of clean water and sanitation

2009
Vaccination against cervical cancer

1970s
Government campaign for healthy living

1948
NHS

1940
Diphtheria vaccination campaign

1896
Microbes identified

PUBLIC HEALTH

MEDICAL KNOWLEDGE, TREATMENT AND PREVENTION

1905
Liberal government welfare reforms

1900

1875
Public health act

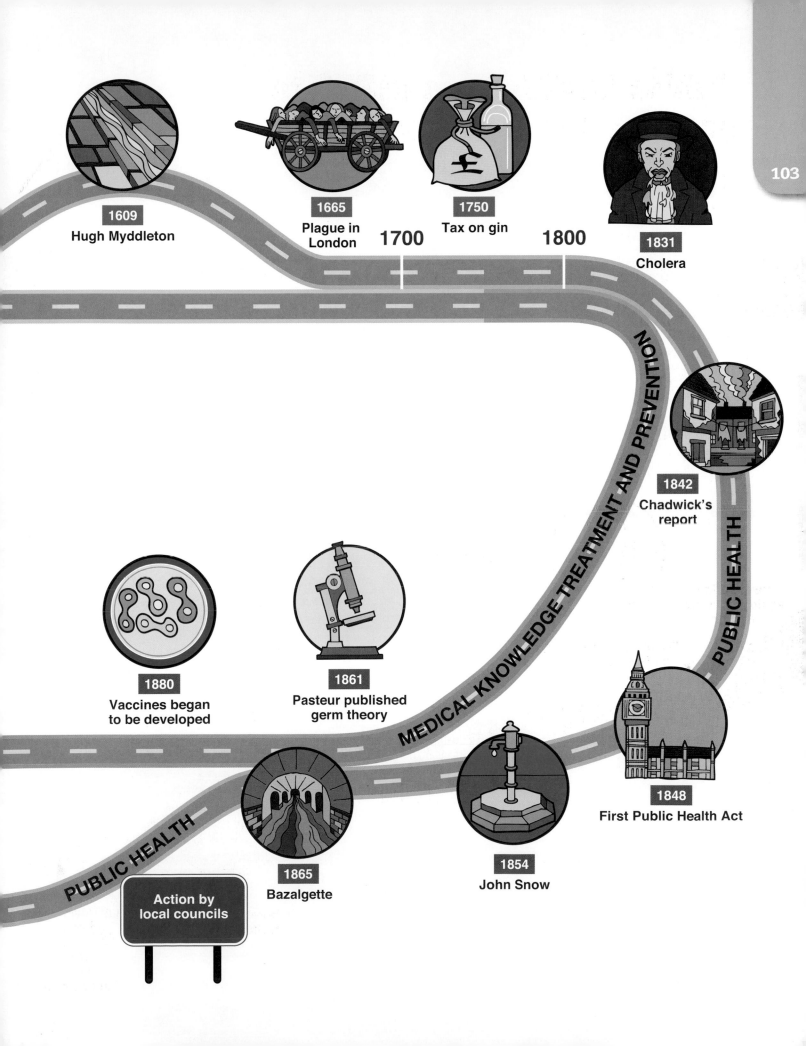

1609
Hugh Myddleton

1665
Plague in London

1750
Tax on gin

1700

1800

1831
Cholera

MEDICAL KNOWLEDGE TREATMENT AND PREVENTION

PUBLIC HEALTH

1842
Chadwick's report

1880
Vaccines began to be developed

1861
Pasteur published germ theory

1848
First Public Health Act

1854
John Snow

PUBLIC HEALTH

1865
Bazalgette

Action by local councils

Introduction

This section extends the core topic by looking at a parallel aspect of medicine in the same period as the core. The same issues are there – what changed and why, what stayed the same, how much progress was made – but covering the topic of public health. You will be asked the same sort of questions as in the core and you may also be asked to link this section with the core and use your knowledge of the wider context to help explain events in public health, or assess their importance.

There will only be one question (of two parts) set on this topic so you need to make sure you have covered the whole specification and you are prepared for the sort of question that is asked.

Part (a) is usually a straightforward question, asking about the key features of something, while part (b) will ask you for some evaluation or judgement. The (b) question will also have three bullet points that remind you to cover all aspects of the question. By themselves, these bullet points will not be enough to answer the question but they should start you thinking about actions that changed government public health provision. So you are being guided towards the coverage that you need to answer this question well, but you also need to think of other examples and use them all to make a judgement. This sort of question does not usually have a 'right' answer – if you make a judgement and back your comments up with supporting evidence, you will get good marks.

Checklist

The key themes are:

● the problems of public health and the attempted solutions, for example the difficulty in providing clean water for the growing population of London

● the particular importance of industrialisation and the increasing amount of government action, for example, the Public Health Acts of 1848 and 1875

● the changing role of the government and different types of public health provision, for example, the growth of the Welfare State in the 20th century.

● the role of factors in the developments in medicine, for example the importance of individuals such as Chadwick and Bevan, and the importance of technology in creating systems to provide clean water and deal with sewage

● the extent of progress within public health provision.

Support activity

You may find it helpful to do a summary chart of the key events, as was suggested in the core section KnowZone, but an alternative approach would be to do a series of ideas maps similar this one:

| Problems caused by growth of industrial towns | Public Health Acts 1848, 1875 |

Public health in the 19th century

| Work of Chadwick, Snow, Farr, Lloyd George | Changing attitudes towards the role of government |

Exam style questions

(a) Why were living conditions in industrial towns so unhealthy in the early 19th century? (9 marks)

(b) How different was the public health provision in the 19th and 20th centuries? (16 marks)

- In 1875 a Public Health Act was passed
- In 1941 a vaccination programme against diphtheria was introduced
- In 1948 the National Health Service was set up.

⭐ **ResultsPlus**
Maximise your marks

(b) How different was the public health provision in the 19th and 20th centuries? (16 marks)

Student answer	Examiner comments	Improved student answer
The standard of public health in the 19th century was very poor. People lived in dreadful conditions and did not have clean water or proper toilets. It is not surprising that there was a lot of disease and when cholera arrived in Britain in 1831, it killed thousands of people.	So far, this is not directly answering the question and therefore has not gained many marks.	The first Public Health Act in the 19th century was in 1848 and it allowed town councils to take action to improve hygiene and to set up Medical Officers, but it did not force them to do this. The 1875 Public Health Act said that town councils were required to provide clean water, drainage and sewerage.
People were shocked when the bad conditions were publicised and so the government decided to take action. A Public Health Act was passed in 1875 that began to improve the provision of public health, and then more action was taken in the 20th century when a vaccination programme was carried out. In the 20th century, the NHS was set up by the government. This offered free health care to everyone, so they could see the doctor, get spectacles and dental treatment and go to hospital, all without paying.	This section of the answer repeats the information in two of the bullet points but then also offers some relevant detail about the NHS. However, it does not make any comparison with the 19th century.	These acts were important but the government provision of public health was just focused on preventing disease through improving hygiene. In the 20th century, the government went further because the acts of 1902–1911 tried to improve people's health by making sure they had access to health care and by providing health visitors and free school meals to improve children's health. The government also encouraged people to have vaccinations against diseases such as diphtheria.
In conclusion, the biggest difference is that in the 19th century government provision was limited whereas in the 20th century it covered a whole range of aspects of public health.	The conclusion begins to make a comparison between the 19th and 20th centuries, but there are not enough details in the essay to support the conclusion. The answer would receive a Level 2 mark (between 5 and 8). Because it has very little extra knowledge and does not make a proper comparison, it would receive a low mark within the level – 6 marks.	In 1948, when the NHS was set up, government provision of public health became even wider. People now had access to a wide range of medical treatment and care, which was given freely, for example they could see the doctor, get spectacles or dental treatment, go to hospital and see a consultant or have an operation. Therefore the provision of public health in the 20th century was on a much bigger scale but also covered a wider range of areas than in the 19th century.

The transformation of surgery c1845–c1918

Introduction

This examination unit looks at a key period in surgery, when major changes were made. It is also the unit in this examination where your understanding of source enquiry skills is tested. This section of the book will therefore give you information about advances in surgery during this period and each section will also be followed by work that will help you to develop your source enquiry skills.

The examination questions in this unit usually follow a pattern testing the following skills:

- inference
- portrayal
- source analysis
- source evaluation for reliability or utility
- cross referencing of sources
- using sources and own knowledge to make a judgement.

The coverage of source enquiry skills in this section of the book will follow a similar pattern.

Source A: An etching of an operation in 1793 by Rowlandson.

Source B: A carbolic spray, used to prevent infection during an operation in the 1870s.

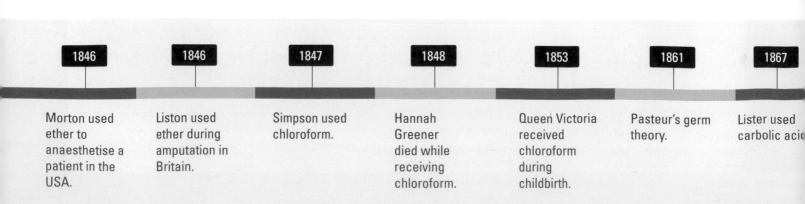

1846	1846	1847	1848	1853	1861	1867
Morton used ether to anaesthetise a patient in the USA.	Liston used ether during amputation in Britain.	Simpson used chloroform.	Hannah Greener died while receiving chloroform.	Queen Victoria received chloroform during childbirth.	Pasteur's germ theory.	Lister used carbolic acid

Source C: A photograph of an operation in 1900.

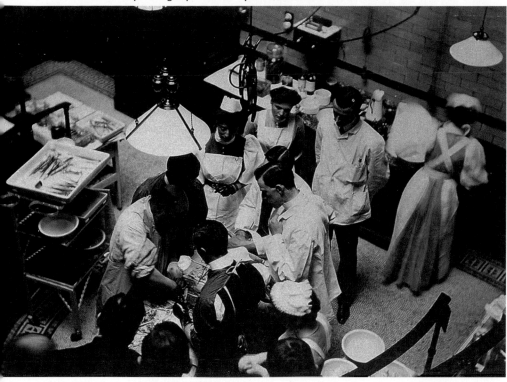

Far from being a respected medical person, the surgeon in the Middle Ages was usually a barber – who happened to do surgery as well because he had a collection of sharp knives! Right up to the late 20th century, a traditional barber's shop used to have a red and white striped pole outside, which symbolised blood and bandages, to remind people that they also used to do surgical operations.

Although surgery had become more scientific by the end of the 18th century thanks to the work of John Hunter (see page 26), people usually had to be desperate before they agreed to have an operation. They knew they would suffer great pain, and many patients died during an operation. However, even if they survived the operation, many patients still died later from infection or blood loss.

Source D: A barber's shop showing a red and white striped pole.

Activities

1 Look at Rowlandson's picture of an operation at the end of the 18th century. What effect do you think this picture would have on someone who needed surgery?

2 Now look at the picture of an operation in 1900. How many changes can you identify?

1877	1878	1901	1905	1916	1916
Lister became Professor of Surgery at King's College Hospital, London, and publicised his ideas about antiseptics.	Koch developed the steam steriliser.	Landsteiner identified blood groups.	Novocaine used as an anaesthetic.	Rous and Turner developed a way of storing blood.	Gilles set up a plastic surgery unit at Aldershot.

6.1 Surgery and anaesthetics in the 19th century

Learning outcomes

By the end of this topic you should be able to:

- understand and explain some of the problems involved in surgery
- explain the importance of speed in operations and understand that this need for speed caused further problems

Amputation: The cutting off of a limb – for example, an arm or a leg – from the body

Anaesthetic: A substance that affects your nervous system so that you are less aware of sensation and don't feel pain

Tourniquet: Something that is tied around a part of the body to put pressure on a blood vessel and stop the loss of blood

The most common sorts of surgical operations in the 19th century were **amputations**, where an arm or leg had to be cut off. This was a fairly straightforward procedure but extremely painful and many people died from blood loss or from infection.

Another operation that was carried out was 'cutting for the stone' in the bladder. This was where there had been some problem inside the body leading to a 'stone' forming inside the bladder, similar to a kidney stone or gall stone. It was an extremely painful condition but since it was in the bladder, it was not deep inside the body. Therefore the surgeon could make a cut at the anus and insert his finger hoping to push out the stone from the bladder. (Kidney stones and gall stones were too far inside the body to be treated.)

Source A: An amputation set from the 19th century.

Saw, to cut through the bone →   ← Knives, to cut through skin, muscles, etc.

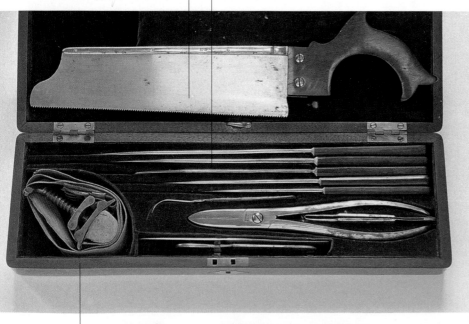

↳ Screw **tourniquet** – the bandage was wrapped around the arm or leg and the screw was tightened so that the flow of blood was stopped while an amputation was being carried out

Until the mid-19th century there were no **anaesthetics**. Patients might be given alcohol, or some form of opium from the poppy to help to ease the pain, but people were often fully conscious during an operation and could feel everything! Because operations were so painful and there were no anaesthetics, they needed to be carried out as quickly as possible and assistants were needed to keep the patient still. Complex operations that took a long time or went deep into the body were impossible and surgery tended to be seen as a last resort.

Source B: A picture of an amputation in the operating theatre of the old St Thomas' Hospital, London, around 1775.

Assistants holding the patient still

Spectators watching

Everyone wearing ordinary clothes

Patient shouting

Sawdust on the floor to soak up the blood

Knives and saw laid out ready for use

Tourniquet around the thigh to stop the flow of blood to the leg

The following source describes the amputation of a leg at the hip joint.

Source C: From an account by Professor James Syme, who was Professor of Surgery at Edinburgh University from 1833 to 1869.

I inserted a narrow knife about a foot long. I cut along the bone, separating it from its socket. Finally I passed the knife around the top of the bone, cutting the remaining ligaments. This ended the operation which had not taken more than one minute.

My assistant slackened the tourniquet around the leg so that we could see how bad the bleeding was. It seemed at first sight as if there were so many blood vessels that they could never all be closed and we knew we must work quickly to prevent the patient's death.

Activities

1 Using Sources A, B and C, make a list of what the sources tell you about the way operations were carried out before anaesthetics were used.

2 Explain why people were so reluctant to have an operation in the early 19th century.

3 Why do you think surgeons did not perform operations on internal organs?

Summary

Operations in the 19th century were very painful and there were no anaesthetics available, so assistants were needed to hold the patient still and the surgeon needed to work quickly. Speed was also important because there was the danger of heavy blood loss, which could lead to death. The problem of infection meant that even if the patient survived the operation, they often died later.

6.2 The discovery of anaesthetics

Learning outcomes

By the end of this topic you should be able to:

- understand and explain the problems caused by the lack of anaesthetics
- explain the importance of the discovery of ether and chloroform

The discovery of an anaesthetic, which would reduce the pain felt by a patient, was a major breakthrough in surgery. It meant the surgeon could work more carefully and take more time if the patient was not struggling – although the problem of blood loss still meant that the surgeon could not take too long.

Date	Event
1799	Humphrey Davy accidentally discovered that inhaling nitrous oxide (also called laughing gas) made you less aware of pain.
1844–1845	Horace Wells, a dentist in the USA, used nitrous oxide when extracting teeth.
1846	William Morton, also a dentist in the USA, found that the gas ether was a more long-lasting anaesthetic. It was used in an operation to remove a growth from a patient's neck. In Britain, Robert Liston used ether while amputating a leg.

There was great excitement at the discovery of anaesthetics but there were also problems in the use of ether.

- It sometimes made patients vomit.
- It tended to irritate the lungs of patients so that they coughed even when they were unconscious.
- It was highly flammable, which was a dangerous situation when the only form of artificial light was from candles or gas lights.
- It tended to produce very deep sleep, which could last for days.
- It had to be carried in large, heavy glass bottles, which were very difficult for surgeons to carry around with them. (Remember many operations were still carried out in the patient's home.)

James Simpson and chloroform

A young surgeon in Edinburgh, James Simpson, wanted to discover a better anaesthetic than ether. One evening he invited some other doctors to his house, where they experimented by inhaling vapours from various chemicals. After Simpson's wife found them all unconscious, they realised that chloroform was extremely effective and it did not seem to have the negative side effects of ether.

Source A: A drawing of Simpson and his friends, waking up after using chloroform, c1850.

Activity

1. Look at Source A. What do you think the artist is suggesting about the effects of chloroform?
2. What elements of the source have helped you to reach that understanding?

Simpson used chloroform in an operation in Edinburgh as early as 1847, but its use became far more widespread after he came to work in London and especially after Queen Victoria used chloroform during the birth of her eighth child in 1853. However, it was difficult to get the dose of chloroform correct – too little and the patient could still feel pain, but too much could be fatal, as was shown when Hannah Greener, a 14-year-old girl who was having an infected toenail removed, died almost immediately after being given the anaesthetic.

Chloroform affected the heart, and a number of young, physically fit patients died after inhaling it. However, in 1848, John Snow developed an inhaler that regulated the dosage and reduced the number of deaths.

Why did some people not want pain relief?

Not everyone welcomed the use of anaesthetics.

- The Victorians were very religious and some people felt that pain relief was interfering with God's plan, especially as the Bible said that God had told Eve that childbirth would be painful.
- Some people distrusted anaesthetics because they were new and their effects were not fully understood.
- Some doctors felt that it was easier for a patient to die if they had been made unconscious than if they remained awake and struggling.
- The number of patients who died shortly after their operations actually increased (see page 116) when anaesthetics were used, which seemed to prove that there was something wrong with anaesthetics.

The effects of both ether and chloroform tended to remain in the body for some time afterwards, so the search for a better anaesthetic continued. It was found that cocaine was effective for pain relief, but it was addictive. However, in 1884 it was discovered that cocaine could be used as a local anaesthetic – to numb a specific part of the body – instead of a general anaesthetic, which made the patient completely unconscious. In 1905 a more effective version, called Novocaine, was developed to be used as a local anaesthetic.

FASCINATING FACT

In 1942, curare, a South American poison, was used as an anaesthetic. This didn't remain in the body for as long as ether or chloroform so patients recovered more quickly.

James Simpson was the first man to be knighted for services to medicine. When he died in 1870, over 30,000 mourners lined the streets of Edinburgh for his funeral. His family refused a burial in Westminster Abbey in London, but a plaque there is dedicated to him. It says 'To whose genius and benevolence, the world owes the blessings derived from the use of chloroform for the relief of suffering'.

Source B: Snow's chloroform inhaler, invented in 1848.

Activities

3 Why do you think James Simpson's discovery of chloroform is seen as an important advance in surgery when ether had already been discovered?

4 Explain the role of each of the following factors in the search for better anaesthetics:
   a) science and technology
   b) religion
   c) social attitudes.

5 Why did the discovery of anaesthetics still not solve the problem of the surgeon having to work quickly?

Summary

The discovery of an effective anaesthetic was a major breakthrough in surgery since it meant the patient was not in pain, and it was welcomed by many. However, some people were slow to accept the idea of anaesthetics, and there were drawbacks to the use of both ether and chloroform.

6.3 Source enquiry skills: inference and portrayal

Learning outcomes

By the end of this topic you should be able to:

- demonstrate that a source can often provide more information than is stated or shown
- understand the way inferences can be made from sources
- make inferences from sources

In history we often try to squeeze more information from a source than it actually tells us. For example, we like to know how people felt about big events as well as knowing what happened. Inference is the word used to describe something that you have worked out from a source, even though it is not actually stated or shown. The inference can be about the situation in the source or about the message or portrayal that the author or artist wants to convey.

Small details can be very important. If you are looking at a picture source, for example a portrait or a cartoon, you need to think about:

- what details have been included
- what is the centre of attention (and how has the artist made it the centre of attention)
- whether people have been shown interacting with each other
- whether anything has been deliberately missed out.

The examination for Unit 3 will usually start with a question asking you what inferences you can make from a source. To get good marks, you must make sure that you explain which part of the source you have used to make each inference.

Look back at Source A on page 110, the picture of Simpson and his friends. The artist has shown two of them asleep and one just waking up; two are on the floor and their chairs have been overturned. By showing them waking up after being unconscious and looking uncertain, the artist has portrayed chloroform as a very strong and effective anaesthetic. He has also portrayed Simpson as someone who is prepared to take risks and experiment on himself.

Now look at Source C on page 109, Professor Syme's description of an amputation. He says that he used a knife that was about a foot long (30cm) – which suggests he needed to be able to cut deep into the hip joint. The inferences that the blood loss was very heavy and also that he knew that blood loss was a great problem in amputations are supported by his comment that they had to work quickly to close off the blood vessels that were bleeding in order to prevent the patient's death.

Look back to Source B (the picture of an amputation in 1775) on page 109. We can infer from this source that the patient is afraid and that operations were normally painful. The parts of Source B that support this inference are the fact that the patient is still conscious while on the operating table, which suggests he will feel pain. You might also be asked about how the cartoonist has portrayed the operation. You can use details to show that he has deliberately chosen to make the operation seem horrific. The patient is shown shouting and struggling and has to be held down by several people, which would suggest that he was afraid and in great pain.

Activities

1. What can you infer from Source A about the way operations were carried out in the early 19th century?
2. What can you infer from Source B about Mantell's attitude towards the use of ether?
3. What can you infer from Source C about people's attitudes towards Simpson and the discovery of anaesthetics?

Source A: A painting from 1817 showing an operation in a patient's home in Dublin to remove a tumour from a man's armpit.

Source B: From the diary of Gideon Mantell, a surgeon.

1 May 1847

Went to Bartholomew's Hospital and witnessed two operations under the influence of Ether: the first I have seen. The loss of feeling on both occasions was complete: the patient had no consciousness of the operation. But the effect on the patient afterwards was appalling, although brief.

Source C: A statue of James Simpson that was erected in Edinburgh after his death; the money for the statue came from collections from the public.

What can you infer from Source A about the way operations were carried out in the early 19th century? (6 marks)

■ **Basic, Level 1 (1 mark)**
Answer describes the picture or explains how operations were carried out.

● **Good, Level 2 (2–3 marks)**
Answer makes a comment about operations, but does not support it from the source.

▲ **Excellent, Level 3 (4–6 marks)**
Answer takes details from the picture and links them to a range of comments about operations.

Summary

An inference is information that can be worked out from a source even if it is not actually stated or shown in the details. Portrayal is about the image or message created by the source. In your answers you should make clear what it is that you have worked out and which part of the source has helped you to make that inference or understand the portrayal.

6.4 Source enquiry skills: source analysis

Learning outcomes

By the end of this topic you should be able to:

- understand how a source creates an overall impression or message

- describe the process of source analysis in order to understand the impression or message

- demonstrate an ability to analyse sources and show how an impression has been created

When you analyse a source, you break it into sections and look at each part separately. You have seen that you need to analyse a source in order to make an inference about the situation or about the author's attitude or purpose. However, sometimes the examination question will tell you what the inference is and ask you to explain how it can be worked out.

For example, this painting of the operation in 1846 when ether was used for the first time deliberately creates the impression that it was an important event.

This extract from the *Boston Daily Evening* newspaper describes the use of ether. As you read it, think about how we can tell that the writer of the article regards the use of ether as a major advance in surgery.

Source A: An extract from the *Boston Daily Evening* newspaper, 1 October 1846.

New and <u>Valuable</u> Discovery

We noticed yesterday the discovery of a new preparation by Dr Morton which is intended to reduce the <u>sufferings of those who are forced to undergo painful operations</u>. The effect of this new discovery is to make the patient unconscious and any <u>operation can then be performed without occasioning</u> pain. We are told by a gentleman of the highest respectability that he witnessed an experiment of the use of this most <u>extraordinary discovery</u> at the rooms of Dr Morton one evening this week. A painful tooth was extracted from the mouth of an individual <u>without giving him the slightest pain</u>. He was put into a kind of sleep by inhaling a portion of this preparation, the effects of which lasted for about three quarters of a minute, just long enough to extract the tooth. This discovery is destined to make a <u>great revolution</u> in the arts of surgery and surgical dentistry.

The contrast between surgery without ether and the effects of ether, e.g. 'the sufferings of those who are forced to undergo painful operations' compared to a state of insensibility where 'any operation can then be performed without occasioning pain'

The use of language to indicate attitude, e.g. 'valuable', 'extraordinary discovery', 'great revolution' all show a positive view of discovery

The deliberate emphasis on the positive effects of ether, e.g. 'without giving him the slightest pain'

Source B: From *The Scientific Revolution in Victorian Medicine* by A. J. Youngson, published in 1979.

Dragged unwillingly, or carried from the ward to the operating theatre by a couple of hospital attendants, the patient was laid on an operating table and, if necessary, strapped down, surrounded by curious strangers. The first cut of the scalpel must have caused searing pain and few patients were able to clench their teeth and remain silent. Shriek after shriek were more likely to fill the room, ebbing away to convulsive cries and sobs as the operation proceeded.

Source C: From a speech by James Simpson to a meeting of doctors in Edinburgh in 1847.

In years to come people will look back with sorrow at our reactions to anaesthetics. They will be amazed at the idea of humane men saying they prefer operating on patients who are conscious instead of anaesthetised, and that the fearful agonies of an operation should be endured quietly.

Source D: A painting showing Dr Morton's use of ether in an operation carried out by Dr Warren in 1846 in the USA.

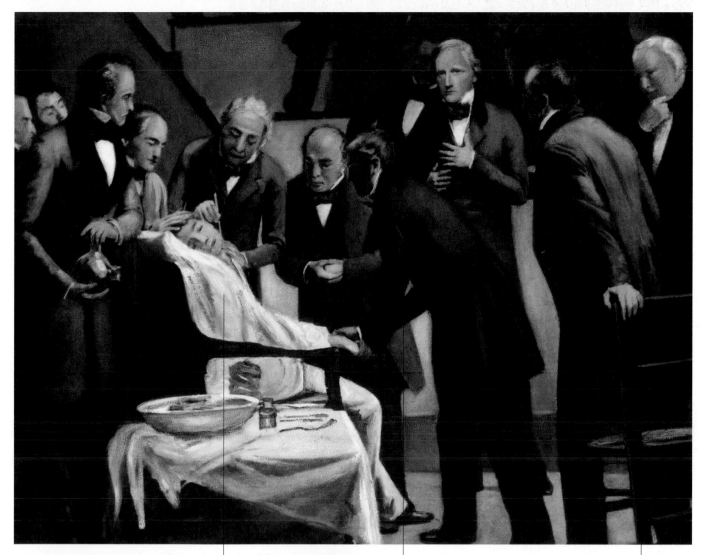

Patient in centre – use of white and of light makes the patient the focus of the painting

Doctors crowding around and bending over the patient suggest concern

Spectators standing up and leaning in to see suggests this is an important event because they want to see the details

Activities

1 Study Source B. How do each of the following points in Source B build up to portray the extreme pain of an operation:

   a) dragged unwillingly

   b) strapped down

   c) searing pain

   d) few patients were able to clench their teeth and remain silent

   e) shriek after shriek

   f) convulsive cries and sobs?

2 How can you tell from Source C that Simpson thought that anaesthetics were an advance in surgery?

Summary

Inference and portrayal are linked to source analysis. You need to look at all the details in the source in order to work out what extra information can be squeezed from the source.

You can work out portrayal from the details the author or artist has chosen to include.

7.1 Understanding infection

Learning outcomes

By the end of this topic you should be able to:

- explain the problem of infection
- understand why the problem of infection became worse after the use of anaesthetics
- understand the reasons why infection could not be dealt with in the mid-19th century

Antiseptic: Something that fights against sepsis and the microbes that create infection

Aseptic: Sterile; free from the microbes that cause infection

Sepsis: A condition in which harmful bacteria affect the flesh, normally leading to infection and decaying flesh

Source B: An example of gangrene.

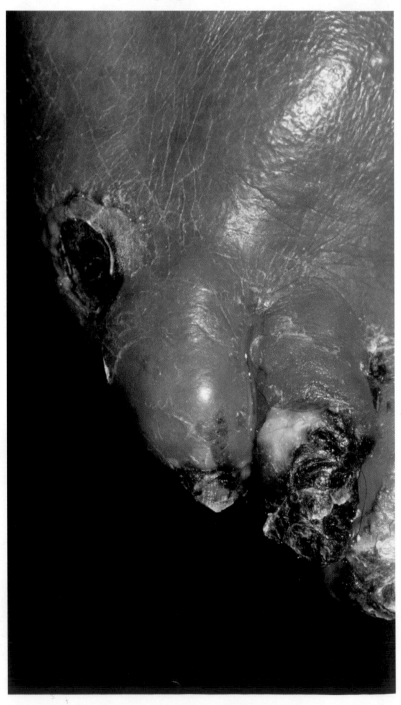

Source: A: From *Lord Lister, his life and work* by G. T. Wrench, 1913.

Getting rid of the dreadful pain which made an operation such a gruesome thing in the past, and which meant that only the most urgent operations were carried out, seemed to open out a new area for surgery. But in hospitals the new 'blessing' of anaesthetics also led to its own defeat. More operations were undertaken for smaller problems, and the dreadful problems of infection and gangrene swept through the wards with redoubled fury.

The problem of infection

The use of anaesthetics seemed to be a major breakthrough in surgery, but it created a new set of problems. As you have seen, when the patient was conscious, surgeons had to work quickly and could not do internal operations that would take a long time; but the use of anaesthetics meant that surgeons could take longer, and they began to do more complex operations. However, they did not understand about infection and germs, therefore many patients survived the operation but died a few days later from gangrene or **sepsis** – infection and decay that produced a strong smell of rotting flesh.

Operations were often carried out in the patient's home or the hospital ward but, even if they were done in an operating theatre, the conditions were not hygienic. Medical students would come to watch and there would be dressers (who held the patient down) all wearing their normal clothes. The surgeon would wear 'special' clothes – usually his oldest coat, with large amounts of dried blood and pus on it, which was seen as a sign that the surgeon was experienced. He might wash his hands in water but the instruments and the operating table would be dirty and unhygienic. Look back at Source B and read Source C on page 114 to remind yourself about the conditions in which operations were carried out. In these conditions it was not surprising that many patients died from infection.

There was still the problem of blood loss, which resulted in the death of many patients. All this meant that the number of deaths linked to surgery actually increased in the 1850s–1870s, and historians sometimes call this the 'Black Period' of surgery.

Early attempts to control infection

Ignaz Semmelweiss worked at Vienna General Hospital in Austria. In 1846 he was concerned that the death rate among women in childbirth was higher in the hospital, in the ward where medical students were involved, than in home births or in wards where midwives delivered the baby. The medical students often came straight from the dissecting room, where they were cutting dead bodies, to the childbirth delivery room. Semmelweiss found that making the students wash their hands using a chlorinated solution reduced the death rate dramatically.

Despite the change in the death rate, many other doctors made fun of Semmelweiss's ideas. He was sacked from the hospital and eventually left Vienna.

James Simpson copied Semmelweiss's ideas when he was Professor of Midwifery at Edinburgh University and later, when he came to London, these methods were not widely accepted for some time.

Meanwhile Florence Nightingale set high standards of hygiene in her work in hospitals and the training of nurses – for example, she insisted on only one patient in each bed.

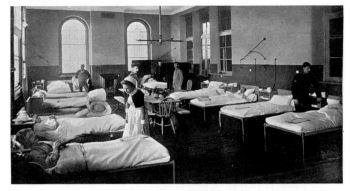

Source C: A ward at Netley Hospital in the late 19th century, showing the emphasis that was being placed on hygiene.

However, Nightingale did not actually understand how infection occurred. She believed in the miasma theory – that disease was caused by poisonous vapours. In fact, the idea of miasma and another idea – that oxygen in the air encouraged infection – led to wounds being tightly bandaged up, something that we now know keeps the temperature high and encourages the growth of bacteria. Consequently, the problem of infection in surgery had still not been solved.

Activities

1 Explain what Source A means when it says 'more operations were undertaken for smaller problems'.

2 Explain why the 1850s–1870s were called the 'Black Period' in surgery.

3 What can you infer from Source C about hygiene in this hospital ward?

4 Think about how operations were carried out and explain why Nightingale's emphasis on cleanliness and hygiene in the hospital wards would not have a big effect on the death rate after surgery.

Summary

Surgeons carried out a greater range of operations after the discovery of anaesthetics and they became more willing to carry our internal operations. However, because infection and microbes were not properly understood, the surgeon and his tools were likely to introduce infection into the wound and so the death rate from operations actually increased.

7.2 Joseph Lister and antiseptics

Learning outcomes

By the end of this topic you should be able to:

- show how Lister overcame the problem of infection
- demonstrate an understanding of how Lister's work led to progress in surgery
- understand the significance of Lister's work within the overall development of surgery

It was not until 1861 that the French chemist Louis Pasteur conducted experiments that proved that decay and infection were caused by microbes in the air. It took time for Pasteur's ideas to be accepted by scientists and even longer for the ideas to be applied to medicine and for surgeons to reach a proper understanding of infection.

Joseph Lister's use of carbolic acid

Joseph Lister was appointed Professor of Surgery at Glasgow University in 1859 and then became Surgeon at Glasgow Royal Infirmary in 1861. He was put in charge of a new building at the hospital. There was hope that the high death rate after operations could be reduced, but this did not happen. Between 1861 and 1865 half of the people who had operations died from infection.

> Lister tried various methods to encourage wounds to heal cleanly, without infection, but had little success.

⬇

> He became interested in Pasteur's work and especially the idea that microbes were responsible for infection in a wound.

⬇

> In 1864 he found that carbolic acid was used in the sewage works at Carlisle and that it killed parasites.

⬇

> Lister thought that carbolic acid could also be used to kill the microbes causing infection.

In 1865 he tested his ideas when an 11-year-old boy was brought into hospital with a compound fracture of his leg. In a compound fracture, the bone pokes through the skin, creating an open wound, and at this time, infection would, almost inevitably, lead to death. Lister soaked the bandages in carbolic acid and watched the wound carefully – there was no sign of pus or infection and at the end of six weeks the fractured bone and the wound had healed.

Source A: Lister's own description of the treatment, from a letter to his father in 1866.

> Though I hardly expected any success I tried carbolic acid on the wound to prevent the formation of pus in the leg. Well it is now eight days since the accident and the patient has reacted just as if there had been no open wound.

Source B: A modern drawing showing Lister using carbolic spray in one of his earliest antiseptic surgical operations, c1865.

The spread of antiseptics

Lister now used a solution of carbolic acid to clean wounds, equipment and bandages, and in 1867 he announced that his wards had been free from sepsis for nine months. In 1877 he became Professor of Surgery at King's College Hospital in London and shortly afterwards carried out an operation on a kneecap under antiseptic conditions. This operation was widely publicised and other surgeons began to copy his methods.

> **FASCINATING FACT**
>
> Listerine was first produced in 1879 as a surgical antiseptic and was named in honour of Lister. In 1895 it was given to dentists for oral care and began to be sold to the public in the USA in 1914.

Lister's other achievements

At this time, silk was used as sutures (or stitches) to sew wounds closed, but there were two problems that caused infection.

- Silk did not absorb carbolic acid and therefore could not be sterilised.
- A thread had to be left dangling out of the wound so that the stitches could be pulled out once the wound had healed.

Source C: A photograph of an operation in the 1880s; the man on the right is operating a carbolic spray.

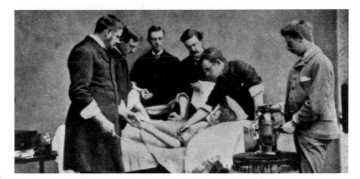

Lister introduced the use of catgut, which could be sterilised, and this reduced the chance of infection. He also developed a form of catgut that would dissolve after several days in the body, so there was no need to leave a thread dangling.

In recognition of the importance of all his work, Lister was given the title of baronet in 1883 and became Baron Lister in 1897. After Lister's death in 1912 a funeral service was held at Westminster Abbey and a fund was set up to organise lectures and statues in his honour. The Lister medal is the highest honour that can be given to a British surgeon.

Activities

1. Explain two ways in which Lister overcame the problem of infection.
2. Explain why Lister's work was such an important advance in surgery.
3. Explain the role of each of the following factors in Lister's development of antiseptics:
   a) chemistry (especially the use of carbolic acid)
   b) technology (especially the work needed to create a spray of carbolic acid during operations).
4. What evidence is there that the importance of Lister's work was recognised by both the medical profession and the public?

Summary

Lister's work in showing the importance of antiseptic conditions was an important breakthrough in surgery, although it took time to be fully accepted.

7.3 Reactions to Lister's antiseptics

> ## Learning outcomes
>
> By the end of this topic you should be able to:
> - explain the various reasons why there was opposition to Lister's ideas
> - understand the gradual shift from antiseptic to aseptic surgery

Although Lister's ideas were quickly accepted in Germany and the USA, many doctors in Britain were unconvinced at first and joked about 'Mr Lister's germs'. Meanwhile others accepted the basic idea of antiseptics but found the whole procedure too difficult or uncomfortable to put into practice especially as carbolic acid made the skin on their hands cracked and sore.

ResultsPlus
Watch out!

Some students assume that new discoveries were quickly accepted by everyone and that people who were slow to accept new ideas were stupid in some way. Many developments in surgery, such as the use of anaesthetics and antiseptics, were opposed at first and this opposition was based on a range of points, which included some valid ideas.

Opposition to Lister's ideas

There was a great deal of opposition to Lister.

- Some doctors didn't accept the idea that microbes caused infection because microbes could not be seen without a microscope.
- Using carbolic solutions slowed down the whole operation, which could lead to problems of blood loss.
- Doctors who copied Lister's ideas did not always copy them properly and then, if they did not get an improved survival rate after operations they said that Lister's ideas were wrong.

- Lister himself kept changing his methods in an attempt to further improve his work – many doctors thought this meant he was not sure of his ideas.
- The equipment was expensive and heavy.
- Some surgeons had good results even without using carbolic acid.
- The nurses resented the extra work caused by this emphasis on hygiene.

However, in 1878 the German doctor Robert Koch identified the bacterium that causes blood poisoning and this helped to convince many people that Lister was right and that microbes do cause infection. In 1878 Koch developed the use of a steam steriliser to ensure that instruments were free from germs.

FASCINATING FACT

Nurse Caroline Hampton, who assisted the American doctor William Halstead, had severe eczema on her hands and carbolic acid was making it worse. In 1890 Dr Halstead asked Goodyear Rubber Company to make rubber gloves for her. A side effect of this was that scientists found out that wearing rubber or latex gloves helped to prevent bacteria being introduced into the wound by the surgeon's hands.

By 1890 most operations were carried out in antiseptic conditions and more complex procedures were undertaken. For example, in the 1880s an infected appendix was removed and in 1896 a surgeon repaired a heart that had been damaged by a stab wound.

Source A: From the memoirs of a doctor who worked with Lister.

Everything was soaked in carbolic – hands, instruments and the patients' skins. The whole scene of the operation was covered in its spray, which dispersed its globules into every nook and cranny of the wound. Our faces and coat sleeves often dripped with it. It was a relief to us all when the spray was [not used anymore]. It was costly and cumbersome and often broke down.

Source B: An operation in *antiseptic* conditions in 1900.

Nurses and surgeons wearing clean white aprons and shirts

Nurses wearing hats to keep hair tidy and prevent infection

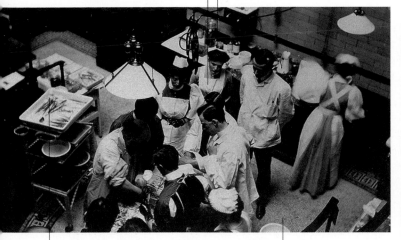

Instruments laid on a clean tray

Bowls so that dirty equipment can be moved away and cleaned afterwards

From antiseptic to aseptic

Developments such as rubber gloves were part of the shift from antiseptic methods (fighting infection and killing bacteria) to **aseptic** conditions, where doctors tried to prevent bacteria being anywhere near the wound. The use of masks, sterile equipment and closed operating theatres are all part of aseptic surgery.

Source C: A modern operation in *aseptic* conditions.

Surgeons and nurses wearing operating gowns that can be sterilised

Surgeons and nurses wearing caps to keep hair tidy and prevent infection

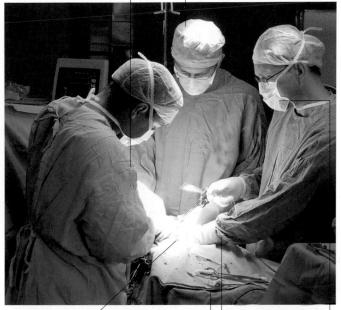

Surgeons and nurses wearing rubber gloves to prevent microbes from their hands getting into the wound or onto the equipment

All instruments sterilised

Sterile cloths to cover all other parts of the body and prevent infection

Surgeons and those close to the operation wearing masks to prevent themselves breathing infection into the wound

Activities

1 Classify the opposition to Lister under two headings: opposition based on scientific thinking; and opposition based on practical problems.

2 Compare Sources B and C. What are the main differences between antiseptic and aseptic conditions?

Summary

Lister's use of carbolic acid as an antiseptic was an important breakthrough in surgery, and once the idea was accepted, the move was made towards aseptic conditions to prevent infection as far as possible.

7.4 Source enquiry skills: reliability

Learning outcomes

By the end of this topic you should be able to:

- understand that sources are not always completely reliable
- explain the factors affecting the reliability of a source
- evaluate the reliability of a source

Source A: A painting of Morton's 1846 operation by the artist Robert Hinckley.

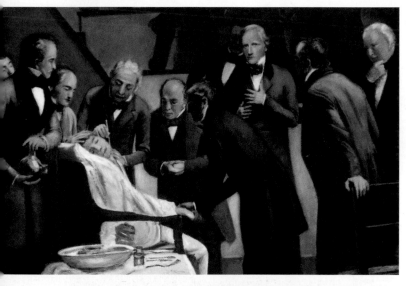

Source B: A photograph of Morton's 1846 operation.

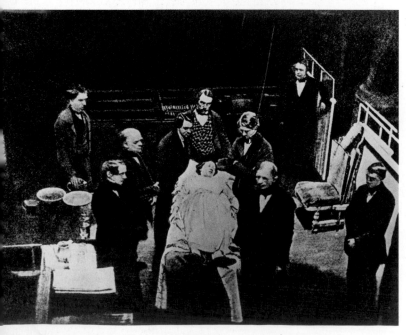

In 1846 Morton used ether to anaesthetise a patient for Dr Warren, who then removed a growth from the patient's neck. Compare the painting of the operation, which you have already studied, to the photograph. The painting by Hinckley was completed in 1892 so you might question whether the artist saw the actual operation and how accurate his memory of it was. If he was not a witness, it would be helpful to know if he had seen the way operations were carried out, if he knew what the people involved looked like or whether the scene was totally made up. You might assume the photograph *must* be reliable – until you find out that the team assembled some time later for the photo to be taken, with someone else posing as the patient! There are clues to the fact that the photograph is posed, in the way that the people are grouped so that they can all be seen clearly. The fact that the patient was a different person shows that the photograph was intended to record the succesful team, and it is those details that are most likely to be reliable. This shows how important it is to consider origins and intentions when you evaluate a source.

Before any source can be used, the historian always needs to evaluate its reliability by considering certain points. These will include the content and selection of the source, its origins, intentions and nature, as well as the language used. There is a more detailed list of these factors on page 130.

An important thing to remember in your answer is to focus on the specific source. Newspapers may sometimes exaggerate and sensationalise their accounts in order to make them interesting and sell more copies – but this is not a relevant comment unless you can provide precise examples from the source to support your comment.

Look back to Source A on page 114. The writer of this article says ether is 'destined to make a great revolution', but his article gives a very factual description with little extreme language, and also emphasises that he got the information from someone of the 'highest respectability' who personally witnessed the use of ether. This newspaper account has not been sensationalised.

Biased sources

A source is likely to reflect the opinion of the author – not many people would bother to write about an event if they didn't have some sort of opinion about it! But that doesn't mean the source is automatically unreliable. You need to decide if the writer's feelings are so strong and his account is so one-sided that the source cannot be trusted, in which case it is biased. Remember that if you say a source is biased you must always explain how that bias has affected the account (for example, whether it is biased in favour of Lister, giving him more credit than he deserves, or if it is biased against him, saying that Lister's achievement wasn't really important). You also have to be able to back up your comments with evidence of loaded language, exaggerations or factual inaccuracies.

Source C: From Knut Haeger, *An Illustrated History of Surgery*, published in 1988.

> Many of Lister's colleagues laughed at him, and Hughes Bennett, a professor of medicine in Edinburgh, asked scornfully 'Where are these little beasts? Show them to us and we shall believe in them. Has anyone seen them yet?' But Lister never bothered to reply and it is said that he only heaved an occasional sigh at the world's stupidity.

It is very clear from Source C that Haeger sympathises with Lister against Bennett. You might feel you want to check whether there is evidence in another source about Bennett's attitude towards germs so that you can be sure about his reaction to Lister's ideas. Alternatively, you might think that Lister may not have been quite as patient as Haeger suggests. However, there is no reason to think that Haeger's sympathy is so strong that it makes this source biased and unreliable.

Source D: A biography of Joseph Lister, taken from the 'discoveries in medicine' website.

> Joseph Lister (1827–1912) developed antiseptic surgery, saving innumerable patients from the dreadful pain and death of post-surgical infection by ensuring that surgical wounds were sterile. As a surgeon, Lister became increasingly disturbed by the high rate of often fatal infections that developed in his patients after surgery. After reading some of **Louis Pasteur**'s findings, Lister concluded that the germs described by Pasteur as being carried in the air caused wound infections. As a result, Lister developed a method to destroy these organisms using carbolic acid as an antiseptic.
>
> Lister first used his new antiseptic surgical technique in March 1865. Although this and many subsequent operations proved the effectiveness of Lister's method to prevent infection, Lister's ideas were opposed by many of his fellow physicians, who thought the antiseptic procedures ridiculously complicated and unnecessary.
>
> In 1877 Lister became a professor at London's King's College Hospital, where he continued to promote his antiseptic methods. Eventually the medical community was won over by his success. By the late 1870s and 1880s, Lister had gained many honours and was a greatly respected figure.

Activities

1 Explain why each of the following is not automatically reliable:
 • a photograph
 • an eyewitness account.

2 Explain how an account written 100 years after an event, such as a historian's book, can still be a reliable source.

3 What examples of 'loaded language' can you find in Source D? How does the arrangement of the details in the source build up to create a positive impression of Lister? Is there anything negative said about Lister?

Summary

The reliability of a source is affected by a range of different factors but very few sources are totally reliable or totally unreliable. In the examination you need to decide how far a source is reliable and to be able to show how you reached your judgement.

7.5 Source enquiry skills: cross-referencing

Learning outcomes

By the end of this topic you should be able to:

- understand that the reliability of a source can be checked by comparing it to another source
- identify points of similarity and of difference when two sources are compared
- weigh up the similarities and differences between two sources in order to reach a judgement on reliability

Historians frequently compare and cross-reference sources to check their accuracy. For example, Source A, an account from a medical student, suggests that there was a very poor standard of hygiene and antiseptic procedures in surgery at the hospital where he worked. How far do Berkeley Moynihan's recollections in Source B support this view?

Source A: A medical student describes the situation in the 1870s.

Often there was an empty ward, with a little notice pasted upon the glass door: 'Ward closed for cleaning'. We knew what that meant, an outbreak of blood poisoning. We students were allowed to go from the dissecting room to attend midwifery cases. True, there was a faded notice saying 'Gentlemen who are dissecting should wash their hands in chlorinated soda solution before going to their cases' but I never knew of anyone doing it, and we did not have the least idea of the reason for the notice.

I remember the house-surgeon with his threaded needles dangling from his coat, which was faded with age, stained with blood and spotted with pus.

Source B: Sir Berkeley Moynihan recalling his education at Leeds in 1888.

The surgeon arrived and threw off his jacket in order to avoid getting blood or pus on it. He rolled up his shirt sleeves and put on an ancient coat which was stiff with old blood. The coat cuffs were rolled up to just above the wrists, and the surgeon washed his hands in a sink and then rinsed them in carbolic acid solution.

When you cross-reference sources you need to follow certain steps to make sure it is done properly.

- Have a clear idea of what it is you want to check in the first source (list the details you are checking).
- Check the second source to see what it says about each of those details. Are they confirmed, challenged or just not mentioned?
- What attitude is shown in the first source? Is it positive or negative? Does it stress any particular aspect?
- Check the attitude of the second source. Is it similar or different?
- Look at the differences between the sources. Are they small differences, for example in numbers, or big differences that might even contradict each other?
- Weigh up the importance of the similarities and differences between the two sources.

It can also be helpful to draw a table, especially if you are cross-referencing more than two sources. You can then compare the sources and see how much support there is for each point.

So let's see how far Source B supports the idea in Source A that there was a poor standard of hygiene and little understanding of antiseptics.

Detail from student's account	Supported, contradicted or not mentioned by Moynihan	Significance of this
Cases of blood poisoning	Not mentioned	Doesn't mean A is unreliable
Use of chlorinated solution as an antiseptic	Surgeon washed his hands in carbolic solution	Supports the idea that they knew about using antiseptics
Students did not understand importance of antiseptics and did not follow procedures	Students not mentioned; surgeon did follow procedures	Even if the surgeon followed procedure it doesn't mean that it is unreliable about the students
Surgeon operated wearing an old coat	Supported; Moynihan stresses how old it was and that it was stiff with blood	Surgeon wearing unhygienic clothes is supported from B

Next think about whether these differences are important.

- Very few details from A are clearly supported from B except the point about the surgeon's clothes. Both sources show an understanding of the need for antiseptics even though different points are mentioned
- The sources show different levels of understanding of antiseptics – the student didn't understand the idea behind it and didn't follow procedures, whereas the surgeon washed his hands and then used carbolic acid.
- However, the surgeon's understanding didn't go very far because he still wore a dirty old coat.

Now you need to decide how far your conclusion is affected by the fact that the sources are about two different places and the fact that Moynihan is talking about a period 10 years later than the student's account.

Your conclusion might be:

Overall, Moynihan's account supports the idea that surgeons operated in dirty clothes. The fact that surgeons did this even when they used carbolic acid suggests that the use of antiseptics was quite new and not properly understood. This makes the rest of the student's account seem likely to be true.

Activities

1 Study Sources A and B. Which source do you feel gives the most reliable account of the standard of hygiene at this time? (Explain your answer.)
2 Look back to the spread 'Reactions to Lister's antiseptics' (pages 120–121) and cross-reference Sources B and C on page 121. How far do they show Lister's ideas being put into practice?

Challenge

3 Why would you need to look at the origins and reliability of both the sources used in cross-referencing? (Clue: why is it important to know whether the sources came from different places or different times? Would it matter if the authors of two sources were linked in some way?)

Summary

It is very rare to find a source that totally agrees with another, so you need to make a judgement about how far the second source backs up the first one, based on what you have found in the process of cross-referencing. This includes a careful matching of detail but should also take into account other issues of reliability as well.

8.1 Blood loss

Learning outcomes

By the end of this topic you should be able to:

- understand how the problem of blood loss was overcome
- identify the key stages in dealing with the problem of blood loss
- evaluate the role played by war, science and technology in overcoming the problem of blood loss.

Cautery: The use of heat to seal blood vessels and stop bleeding

Ligature: A thread tied around a blood vessel to stop bleeding

Transfusion: The process of giving blood from a donor to the patient

Source A: A description of surgery in the 1840s by Dr Abbot. This describes an operation in the US but the same procedure would have taken place in Britain.

I remember an operation upon a young man for the removal of a large cancerous growth on the end of his tongue. The operation was done by a short, quick stroke of a knife which removed the outer half of the tongue. Of course, the bleeding was quite free. Dr Warren stepped back to the furnace where the hot iron was. At a look from Dr Warren the assistant quickly slipped both of his hands over the patient's eyes and the hot iron was instantly applied to the whole bleeding surface of the tongue. The patient jerked suddenly backwards. Driven almost insane by the pain and the sizzle of his searing flesh, the patient broke free from his restraint, and a bloody struggle ensued with the attendants who attempted to hold him down.

Blood loss has always been a major problem in surgery. Bleeding makes it difficult for the surgeon to see what he is doing, but there is also the problem that if a patient loses too much blood, his blood pressure drops, which affects his heart, and then his body cannot function and he dies. During the 17th century, there were experiments with blood **transfusions** using blood from animals (usually sheep) as well as from humans. Although patients occasionally survived, in most cases they died and the procedure was banned. Once anaesthetics and antiseptics made it possible to perform complex operations, there was a renewed drive to find a way of dealing with the two problems of blood loss.

Controlling blood loss

The usual way to deal with wounds or amputations was to seal the blood vessels by placing a hot iron onto the wound or pouring hot oil over it. This process was called **cautery** and was extremely painful.

In the 16th century a French surgeon, Ambroise Paré, developed metal clips to place on arteries during an operation. He also tried using silk thread to tie the blood vessels after an amputation instead of using heat to seal them. This was far less painful, but the **ligatures** did not always stop the bleeding if they were not tied properly. Furthermore, this was before Pasteur developed the germ theory and therefore there was no understanding of the way that a surgeon's dirty hands inside a wound increased the chances of infection and led to a higher death rate. For these reasons, cautery continued to be the main way of dealing with bleeding until Paré's idea of silk ligatures was further developed by Joseph Lister in the late 19th century.

Source B: Clamp used to stop blood loss during the amputation of a leg.

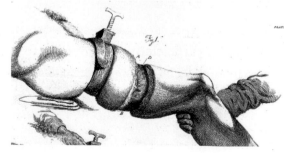

Replacing blood – transfusions

It had therefore become possible to at least partly control the loss of blood during an operation, but the problem of replacing blood was not solved until after 1901 when Karl Landsteiner suggested that there were different blood types – A, B and O; a fourth group, AB, was added in 1902.

Landsteiner showed that blood transfusions had to be between people with the same blood group or else the patient died. However, even with this breakthrough, there was still the problem that a donor needed to be present to provide the blood whenever it was needed. This was not very practical and therefore his work did not have a big immediate effect on surgery.

Source C: A drawing of a 19th-century blood transfusion.

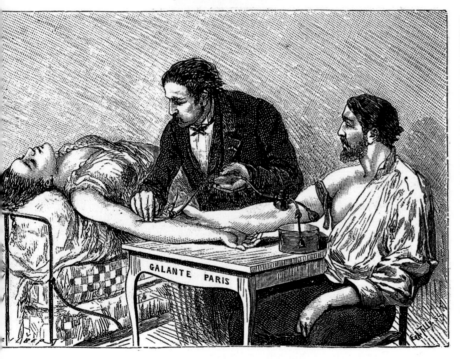

During the First World War (1914–1918) many soldiers died in the trenches from blood loss even when the wound itself was not fatal. As a result, there was a new emphasis on the search for a way to store blood for use at a later date.

- In 1915 the American doctor Richard Lewisohn found that adding sodium citrate stopped blood from clotting. This meant that the donor did not have to be present and therefore more transfusions could be carried out. Although it was found that the blood cells would deteriorate if the blood was not used soon afterwards, this discovery still saved the lives of thousands of wounded soldiers.

- Richard Weil found that this blood could then be stored in refrigerated conditions.
- In 1916 Francis Rous and James Turner found that adding a citrate glucose solution allowed blood to be stored for longer. This meant that when an attack was planned, the army could ask for donations of blood from the public, so that they were available for transfusion to treat the wounded.
- The first blood depot was established in 1917 for the Battle of Cambrai using blood group O, which can be safely given to all patients, whatever their blood type.

Activities

1 Why could transfusions not be used until the 20th century?

2 Explain which was more important in the development of blood transfusions – Landsteiner's identification of blood groups or Rous and Turner's discovery of ways to store blood.

3 Explain which factor had more effect on the development of blood transfusions – science and technology or war.

Summary

Overcoming the problem of blood loss was an important stage in the development of surgery. It depended on increased scientific knowledge but its development was also accelerated by the casualties of war.

8.2 Source enquiry skills: the usefulness of sources

Learning outcomes

By the end of this topic you should be able to:

- understand that the value of a source varies depending on the enquiry
- explain how the usefulness of a source should be evaluated
- evaluate a source's usefulness

Useful information

The usefulness of a source varies according to what the historian is investigating. A diary entry from James Simpson or Joseph Lister might be very helpful if the historian wants to know how they developed their ideas, but it might not have much information about how quickly other doctors accepted their new techniques. For the historian, a patient's account and a doctor's account of the same operation before the use of anaesthetics might be equally useful, but in different ways.

When evaluating a source's usefulness, you need to have a clear idea of how the information in the source relates to the historian's enquiry.

1   When a new technique is used it will create a range of historical sources.

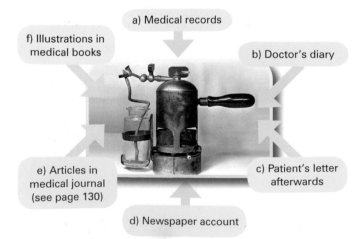

a) Medical records
f) Illustrations in medical books
b) Doctor's diary
e) Articles in medical journal (see page 130)
c) Patient's letter afterwards
d) Newspaper account

2   The historian must be clear what is the focus of the enquiry.

Here are some examples of enquiry questions about a new technique.

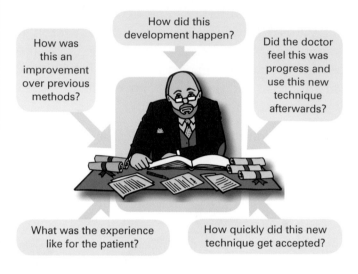

How did this development happen?

How was this an improvement over previous methods?

Did the doctor feel this was progress and use this new technique afterwards?

What was the experience like for the patient?

How quickly did this new technique get accepted?

Both the following sources are about Lister's use of carbolic acid as an antiseptic, but their usefulness depends on the historian's enquiry.

Source A: From a letter from Lister to Pasteur in February 1874.

> ... give thanks for having, by your brilliant researches, proved to me the truth of the germ theory. You furnished me with the principle upon which alone the antiseptic system can be carried out.

Source B: A table based on Lister's own records, showing the death rate among amputation cases before and after the use of carbolic acid.

Years	Total cases	Survived	Died	Death rate
1864 to 1866	35	19	16	46%
1867 to 1870	40	34	6	15%

Source A would clearly be very useful if you wanted to understand the ideas behind Lister's use of carbolic acid. It states that he got the idea from Pasteur's work on germs and there is no reason to doubt this since it comes from Lister himself.

Source B would be very little use for that enquiry but extremely helpful if you wanted to assess the impact of antiseptics on surgery.

Source C: Publicity 'blurb' for a book called *Joseph Lister and the Story of Antiseptics* by John Bankston.

None of the doctors could figure it out. During the nineteenth century, surviving surgery was only half the battle. In many hospitals, 50 percent of amputees lived through their painful operations only to die soon afterwards in their beds. Everyone had a theory for what doctors referred to as 'hospitalism'. But it was not until Joseph Lister and his pioneering work in antiseptic methods that death rates were greatly reduced after surgery. His work is so important that surgical history is divided into two eras: Before Lister and After Lister.

ResultsPlus
Watch out!

Many students think the usefulness of a source depends on how much information it contains, or assume that a source produced at the time is automatically better than a source produced later.

Value of the source

You should consider whether a source has relevant information but also how that information is affected by the source's reliability or nature and origins.

- What sort of information does the source give and how much does it apply to your enquiry?
- Does the source have any added weight because of its origins or intentions? For example, does it come from someone who was involved in the event? Is it an official source?
- If the source gives you only one example, can you assume it is representative of the wider situation? For example, did all doctors feel the same way?

A reliable source is obviously very useful to the historian because it can provide accurate details that can be used to provide an outline of events or to cross-reference other sources. Unfortunately very few sources are completely reliable.

Nevertheless, unreliable sources can still be useful for telling us about attitudes, so the historian needs to weigh up the strengths and limitations of a source every time it is used.

- A diary comes from someone involved; he/she should know what happened but may exaggerate his/her own importance or describe events only from a personal point of view
- A newspaper headline may seem sensationalised or exaggerated in order to sell many copies, but the article should still include factual information and, most importantly, help us to understand what people at the time were likely to be thinking.
- A photograph shows the event as it happened, and very few photographs are faked or falsified, but most photographs have been taken from a particular angle or posed in order to create a certain impression.

Activities

1 Explain the strengths and weaknesses of each of the following types of sources for a historian researching the development of antiseptics:
   a) *official records* of operations carried out in a hospital before and after the use of antiseptics
   b) *private records* from Lister, for example a diary or letters
   c) *a newspaper report* about the new discovery
   d) *a photograph* of Lister operating
   e) *a medical journal article* written by one of Lister's opponents.

2 Test your understanding of the value of sources by using Source C. What suggests that this book sees Lister's work as a positive development and a turning point in surgery and how would that affect the value of this book to the historian?

Summary

Sources are used in different ways depending on the focus of the historian's enquiry. All sources should be evaluated each time they are used.

8.3 Source enquiry skills: comparing the value of sources

Learning outcome

By the end of this topic you should be able to:
- understand the process of source evaluation and comparison

Journal: (1) An account that is written up at regular intervals, like a diary – this is a personal or private source. (2) A published set of articles (like an academic magazine), for example *The Lancet* is a respected medical journal containing articles by doctors and researchers

Primary sources are sources produced at the time, for example a **journal** or diary, a newspaper, hospital records, a photograph, equipment, a building or someone's spoken account. However, they do not always come from people who were involved in the event and they are not automatically 'better' than secondary sources.

Secondary sources are sources produced at a later date and are based on primary sources. Secondary sources can be historical books, paintings, films, museums or websites. They should not be seen as 'second-hand' or 'second-rate' and are often very reliable. Many people at the time wouldn't know the full details of an event, while the historian can have wider knowledge by looking at more sources and be more able to see the event in context.

ResultsPlus
Watch out!

Many students assume that a secondary source must be unreliable because the historian was not there at the time of the event. However, an account written by a historian should actually be very reliable because they have investigated lots of sources and weighed them up in order to write a full explanation.

It is important that the historian uses a wide range of sources in order to balance out the strengths and weaknesses of the sources and get a good understanding of the issue. Of course, the historian may be trying to make a point and therefore might emphasise something or use loaded language,

so you should still treat the account as a source and evaluate it as usual.

The value of sources
- *Content* – What clues are there to show how well the historian understands and has researched the topic?
- *Language* – Are there any examples of loaded language where the historian's attitude might affect the reliability of the source?
- *Origins* – Who is the historian? Do they have expert knowledge? When were they writing and is that important?
- *Intention* – Is the historian writing this for any particular purpose, for example to celebrate 100 years of anaesthetics or to argue with another historian?
- *Nature* – What sort of source is it – part of a series of works, a visual work or even a television documentary?
- *Selection* – Has the historian chosen to focus on one event or one aspect? Has anything been missed out?

Examination questions asking you to compare the value of two sources do not usually have a 'right' answer; they are just testing whether you understand all the issues covered. In very general terms, primary sources tend to focus on individual cases and show the personal feelings and attitudes of the people involved, while secondary sources rarely have that personal element but can give an overview and set events in a wider context, which is vital if you want to look at how successful something was.

Activities

1 Test your understanding in the following exercise.

Study Sources A and B. Which source is most valuable for telling you about people's reactions to the use of chloroform?

Source A: A report in a medical newspaper about the use of chloroform, December 1849.

A Welsh girl had to undergo a very painful operation, the removal of an eyeball. The surgeon administered about one-third of the quantity of chloroform he had given to other patients. It had, however, such an effect on her that she had a fit and died.

Source B: From *For Fear of Pain: British Surgery 1790–1850* by Peter Stanley, 2003.

It is possible that surgeons only used chloroform in the 1850s because patients demanded it. It kept patients from pain.

Activities

Challenge

2 Explain how you would evaluate a visual secondary source, for example a drawing of an operation created for a school textbook.

Answers

There is no right answer to the Activity question, but for high marks you should have taken account of the reliability or nature of the source when you weighed up the usefulness of the information. The points suggested on page 130 may not all be relevant but the sorts of comments an examiner would look for are as follows:

Source A
- It tells us about a death caused by chloroform but does not tell us how people reacted.
- It implies that chloroform was used successfully in other cases.
- It suggests there was a problem deciding on the exact dose.
- The language is neutral and does not appear to be exaggerated.
- Since it is reported in a medical newspaper, it should be accurate because doctors would need to know about cases like this.
- There is no suggestion that this was a common problem or that there was a strong reaction to the use of chloroform.

Source B
- It says it made operations less painful.
- This shows that the public knew about chloroform and wanted it to be used in their operations.
- It suggests the surgeons would not have used chloroform as much if the public had not wanted it.
- The title of the book suggests it has a focus on the development of anaesthetics and therefore should have a good understanding of the whole context.
- The historian is careful to say 'It is possible' – he obviously feels his information is not strong enough to say definitely.
- The historian will have looked at a wide range of sources to make this judgement; there's no reason to doubt it.

Summary

Historians' views must be evaluated in the same way as other sources; they have both strengths and weaknesses. Primary sources are not automatically better than secondary sources. The value of any source depends on how the source context helps the historian while taking account of the source's reliability or nature and origins to see if that gives the source any added weight.

9.1 The role of war in the development of surgery c1845–c1918

Learning outcomes

By the end of this topic you should be able to:

- explain the link between war and developments in surgery
- show an understanding of the role played by war in the development of surgery
- evaluate the role played by war in the development of surgery

Plastic surgery: Surgery carried out in order to change the appearance of the patient

Prosthetic limb: Artificial arm or leg, often made from metal and plastic

In this final section on surgery, you need to look back at the role of various factors and consider what effect they had on developments in surgery – did they make a development possible, speed it up or hold it back?

In the First World War (1914–1918), surgeons often treated wounded soldiers close to the front line of fighting where the difficult conditions and large numbers of injuries put them under immense pressure. Surgeons therefore gained a great deal of experience in a wide range of injuries and sometimes had to improvise new techniques. In this way, war can be said to have accelerated their training.

War

Source A: A field surgery basket containing equipment for surgery to be carried out during a battle in the First World War.

Source B: A painting by Henry Tonks, a surgeon and artist, showing a military dressing station in France in 1918. A dressing station was the place where the injured would receive basic treatment before they were sent to hospital for more complicated treatment.

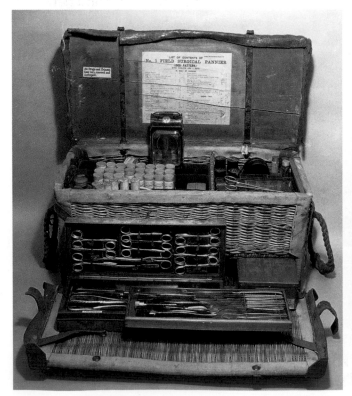

New developments in surgery

- The use of explosive weapons meant that many soldiers suffered deep wounds, and when fragments of clothing entered the wound, it caused infection. Surgeons found that cutting away infected tissue and soaking the wound with a saline (salt) solution was the best way of dealing with this (although they still could not deal with serious infection as antibiotics were not developed until later).
- Surgeons also found themselves having to make early attempts at brain surgery because of the nature of some injuries received in the war.
- At the start of the First World War, the New Zealand doctor Harold Gilles asked for permission to set up a **plastic surgery** unit in the British army.

The development of plastic surgery

```
Before First World        →    Gilles was          →    Gilles began to
War French surgeon             aware of these            experiment with
Morestin worked on             developments              ways of
facial surgery.                and asked for             reconstructing
                               permission to             facial injuries and
                               set up a plastic          paid particular
Before First World War    →    surgery unit in           attention to the
French and German              the British               attempt to create
surgeons were                  army.                      a normal
developing skin graft                                    appearance.
techniques, using tissue
from another part of the
body to repair an injury.
```

```
He kept careful        He developed the new technique of pedicle tubes.
records,               • A narrow layer of skin was lifted up from the
including                body and stitched into a tube at one end.
drawings of the        • The other end was still attached to the body and
injuries and the         this meant blood continued to circulate and
reconstructions          helped healthy skin to develop.
he created.            • When the tube had grown long enough, the free
                         end was attached to the new site.
                       • Once the skin graft was in place, the pedicle tube
                         could be cut free at the base.
```

Activities

1. Draw a topic web summarising the different ways in which war affected developments in surgery.

2. Colour code your topic web to show examples of:

   a) war accelerating developments in surgery

   b) war leading to new developments in surgery.

3. What other factors affecting surgery do you think were linked to the role of war? (Clue: look back to the work on blood transfusions.)

Source C: A photograph of a patient undergoing plastic surgery, showing pedicle tubes being used to graft skin onto the face.

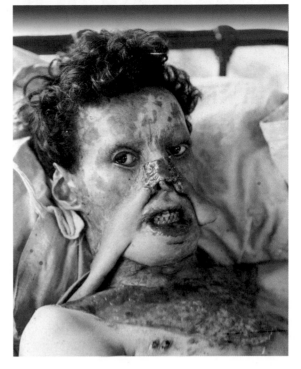

Prosthetic limbs

Between 1914 and 1921 over 41,000 men in the British armed forces lost a limb. Advances in **prosthetic limbs** included the use of light metal alloys and new mechanisms, but there were long waiting lists for these to be fitted and patients then needed training to use them properly.

Summary

War had a big effect on surgery and led to much progress being made. However, it also had the effect of focusing attention on dealing with wounds, and so progress in other areas of surgery, such as the search for better anaesthetics, may have been delayed as a result.

9.2 The role of science and technology in the development of surgery c1845–c1918

Science

Chemistry played an important part in developing anaesthetics and antiseptics. These developments then made surgeons willing to try more complex operations, for example removing tumours. They also began to deal with internal obstructions, such as the hard 'stones' inside the gall bladder formed from cholesterol or pigments from blood cells (an extremely painful condition). In the 1880s operations to remove gallstones and the gall bladder became routine as a result of better anaesthetics and antiseptics. This also led to other procedures being developed to deal with internal problems, for example, the removal of the appendix. Chemistry was also important in the development of a suitable technique to store blood until it was needed for transfusion.

> ### FASCINATING FACT
>
> In 1902 Edward VII was diagnosed with appendicitis. He wanted to delay the operation to remove his appendix because he was due to be crowned at Westminster Abbey the next day but Lister told him, 'In that case, Your Majesty, it will be a corpse that is crowned.'

Infection was controlled by using Lister's carbolic spray, sterilising the instruments, wearing rubber gloves and using sterilised catgut for ligatures. In the move to aseptic surgery, gowns and face masks were also used and the operating theatre was a closed environment. This was all based on Pasteur's work on the germ theory, an understanding of chemistry and biology, and the development of the new science, bacteriology.

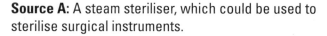

Source A: A steam steriliser, which could be used to sterilise surgical instruments.

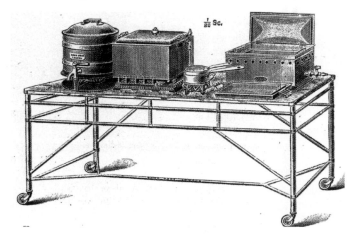

The discovery of X-rays by Wilhelm Roentgen in 1895 made surgeons more confident about internal operations. Roentgen did not take out a patent on his discovery, which meant people were free to copy his ideas. As a result, the use of X-rays spread very quickly – the London Royal Hospital had its first X-ray machine in 1896. X-rays also made it possible for surgeons to extract bullets and shrapnel without having to dig around in a wound, and this reduced the problems of bleeding and infection. The importance was quickly recognised by surgeons, and mobile X-ray units were developed for use during the First World War for the benefit of surgeons working in the front line.

Source B: A modern X-ray showing the chest of someone affected by shrapnel after a bomb blast.

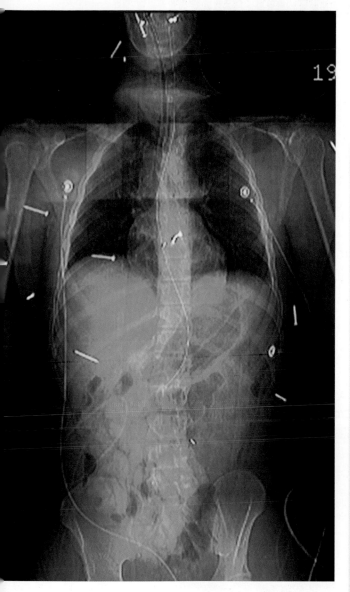

Other important examples of technology helping surgery to advance are the carbolic spray, the steam steriliser, the X-ray machine and the hypodermic needle (invented in 1853 by Alexander Wood) used in blood transfusions.

Source C: A diagram of a late 19th-century hypodermic needle.

Activity

Look at these examples of science and technology linked to surgery. Explain why science by itself would not have had much effect on surgery.

Science	Technology
Improved understanding of anatomy and physiology helped surgeons when they began to do more complex operations.	X-rays were discovered by Wilhelm Roentgen in 1895 and X-ray machines were installed at many hospitals within 10 years.
Experiments were undertaken to find the most effective anaesthetic.	Equipment was developed to deliver anaesthetics and then to measure the dose.
Pasteur's germ theory showed how microbes spread infection.	Carbolic spray, steam sterilised instruments and sterilised catgut all helped to cut down on infection in surgery.
Knowledge of chemistry helped to develop techniques for storing blood to use in transfusions.	The invention of the hypodermic needle in 1853 by Alexander Wood made it possible to measure an injection of a drug or a withdrawal of blood.

Technology

Developments in surgery are closely linked to improvements in scientific knowledge, for example discoveries about germs, anatomy, X-rays and chemicals. However, the role of technology is also very important. When chloroform was first administered, it was usually done by pouring some drops onto a handkerchief for the patient to inhale. As you have seen, it was difficult to get the dosage right and chloroform affected the heart, leading to the death of some patients. Dr John Snow developed an inhaler that was much safer.

Summary

Science played an important role in suggesting ways of improving surgery, but technology was needed to put these ideas into practice.

9.3 The interaction of factors affecting the development of surgery

Learning outcomes

By the end of this topic you should be able to:

- explain the link between individual factors and the development of surgery
- demonstrate the interaction of different factors in the development of surgery
- evaluate the importance of various factors in the development of surgery

The spread of ideas

The emphasis on scientific methods during the 17th and 18th centuries had led scientists to publish their ideas and details of their experiments. During the 19th century many scientific and medical journals, such as the journal produced by the Royal College of Surgeons, encouraged the publication and discussion of new ideas and problems. For example, the death of Hannah Greener from chloroform was reported in the medical journal *The Lancet*.

Pasteur published his germ theory that microbes in the air caused decay and infection and Lister applied this idea to his attempts to reduce infection. In this way, Lister was able to build on Pasteur's work and communication helped surgery to advance.

The reason why surgeons were able to make use of X-rays so soon after Roentgen's discovery was because he published his work and did not take out a patent to prevent other people from copying his ideas.

Surgeons often wanted their work to be recorded. We have both photographs and artwork of several key events, such as the first use of ether, field surgery in the First World War and the work of Gilles in plastic surgery.

The public were also interested in developments in surgery, so the papers reported the first use of anaesthetics, Queen Victoria's use of chloroform and the removal of King Edward VII's appendix.

Sometimes surgeons and scientists would travel to visit each other or to meet for conferences. Lister travelled through Germany and around the USA discussing his ideas. He met Pasteur in Paris in 1892 at a conference of 2,500 scientists, when Lister paid tribute to the importance of Pasteur's work.

Source A: In this painting Pasteur is on the stage, being supported by the President of France.

Nevertheless, communication was not always effective. Lister did not know about the work of Semmelweiss, and Morestin was unwilling to share his ideas on plastic surgery with Harold Gilles.

Individuals

Some of the developments you have studied would probably have happened anyway. The use of ether had been such a breakthrough in surgery that when people realised the problems involved in using it, they did not want to abandon anaesthetics – they just wanted to find a better one. Simpson set out to discover a new anaesthetic, but if he had not discovered chloroform, someone else probably would have done. However, the fact that Queen Victoria's doctor was a friend of Simpson perhaps led to its use on royalty, which then convinced many other people that it was an example of progress.

In the same way, someone else might have discovered how to use carbolic acid instead of Lister, but the fact that he kept careful records, publicised his ideas, tried different methods and was prepared to keep on with his ideas even

when he was ridiculed all helped to get his ideas accepted. (Remember that when Semmelweiss tried to improve hygiene, he was unsuccessful.)

The work of these individuals must also be seen in the context of what else was happening. Lister's ideas were accepted more readily than Semmelweiss's because Pasteur had published his germ theory – but even so, Lister's ideas were accepted in Germany and the USA before they were widely accepted in Britain.

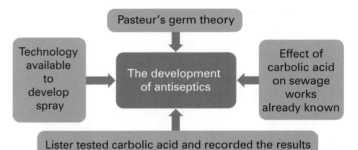

Summary

Various factors were involved in developments in surgery, often interacting with each other, so that war, science, technology and communications all contributed to developments such as blood transfusions.

Activities

1. Explain how good communications have affected progress within surgery and acceptance of new ideas by the public.

2. Draw a picture to show the factors and events involved in the development of (a) aseptic surgery and (b) blood transfusions. You could use the image of a relay race, or a team climbing up a cliff face to show how early developments contributed to later discoveries.

3. How important do you think individuals were in these developments? For example, was so much work being done on anaesthetics that chloroform would have been discovered anyway? Lister was Professor of Surgery at Glasgow University – if carbolic acid had been discovered by someone else, would they have been in a position to publicise it so much?

9.4 Source enquiry skills: making a judgement

Learning outcomes

By the end of this topic you should be able to:

- understand the need to consider several aspects of an issue
- analyse the questions and plan a suitable response

The final question in the examination will always require you to use sources and your own knowledge to make a judgement on an issue about surgery in this period. You may be asked why something happened or how important it was, or to evaluate the role of factors in developments in surgery. You should also remember that in history there is rarely a clear-cut answer – usually you have to weigh up two sides of an issue.

It is important to plan your answer so that you build up a logical argument rather than produce random comments. You also need to make sure that your comments are all supported by points from the sources in the examination paper and from your own knowledge. Study the following example.

Use the sources A, B, C and your own knowledge to explain whether the advance in scientific knowledge was the most important factor in the development of antiseptics.

Start by analysing the question.

- What topic knowledge do you need?
  Facts about antiseptics and Lister.
- What does the question want you to do?
  Explain the factors involved in why antiseptics developed and show which was the most important.
- How do you do it?
  Show the effect of each factor on the development of antiseptics and make a judgement about their importance.

Look at the sources, how can you use them to support your comments?

Source A: From a letter from Lister to Pasteur, February 1874.

I give you thanks for having, by your brilliant researches, proved to me the truth of the germ theory. You furnished me with the principle upon which alone the antiseptic system can be carried out.

Lister is clearly saying that Pasteur's work on the germ theory was the basis for his work on antiseptic techniques.

This suggests science was the key factor.

Source B: From a letter written by Lister to his family shortly after he began at King's College Hospital, London.

The theatre was again well filled and I felt very nervous before the operation, yet I lost all consciousness of the presence of the spectators once I started the operation. Just before I began I remembered that only one Spectator mattered [God] and this thought gave me increased firmness.

The presence of spectators shows Lister is publicising his new technique, hoping that students will use it in their work.

Lister's comments suggest that he was a determined individual and gives an insight into Lister's beliefs and how he is strengthened by his religion to stay focused on surgery.

ResultsPlus

Watch out!

The question will always tell you to use the sources and your own knowledge. The mark scheme will have a cut-off point for answers that do not do this. Every year many students who produce an excellent answer lose marks because they only use the sources and do not add in comments from their own knowledge. There are also a number of excellent answers every year that lose marks because they do not refer to the sources in their answer.

Source C: An illustration from W. Cheyne's book, *Antiseptic Surgery*, published in 1882. The caption gave the instruction: 'The surgeon should always have his hands in the spray and the assistant hands the instruments into the spray.'

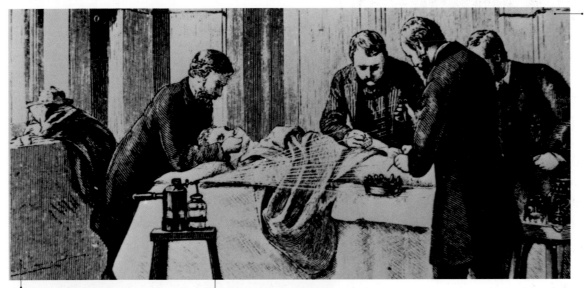

→This shows the importance of communications in spreading ideas (and Source A shows the importance of Pasteur's work being communicated to Lister)

The book tells other surgeons how to use the carbolic spray

└→This shows the importance of technology in making the spray

Now think about your own knowledge. What can you add about how Lister developed carbolic acid as an antiseptic?

Plan your answer.

- We have identified four factors here – science, the individual, technology and communications. You need to explain the role played by each of these in the development of antiseptics.
- When historians try to explain why something happened, they usually talk about a web of causation in which several factors interact, rather than a single chain of events with one thing leading directly to another. You could do a quick diagram to show how the factors involved in the development of antiseptics interacted.

- The question asks if science was the main factor, so in your answer you should try to weigh up each of them – was any one factor so important that antiseptics would not have been developed without it?
- Once you have thought about all the sections of your answer, put them into a logical order so that your answer builds up into a convincing explanation.

Different people could reach very different conclusions here – *and get the same mark!* What matters is your explanation and whether you have backed up your ideas with evidence from the sources and your own knowledge.

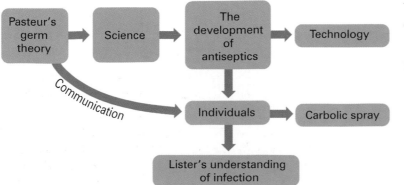

Summary

There is not usually a 'right' answer to these judgement questions, but remember to look at all sides of the issue involved and to back up your answer using evidence from the sources *and* your own knowledge.

9.5 Source enquiry skills: further practice

Use the sources A, B, C and D and your own knowledge to explain who made the greater contribution to the advance of surgery – Simpson or Lister. (16 marks)

Start by analysing the question.

- What topic knowledge do you need?
  Facts about Simpson and Lister.
- What does the question want you to do?
  Compare their importance.
- How do you do it?
  Show the effect of their work on surgery and make a judgement about their importance.

Now look at the sources. How can you use them?

Source A: Charles Darwin's description of an operation in the early 19th century, before the use of anaesthetics.

> I attended the operating theatre and saw two very bad operations… but I rushed away before they were completed. Nor did I ever attend again, for hardly any inducement would have been strong enough to make me do so; this being long before the blessed days of chloroform. The two cases fairly haunted me for many a long year.

Source B: From an article in the medical journal *The Lancet*, 1853.

> A very strange rumour has been spread that her Majesty, Queen Victoria, during her last childbirth, used chloroform, something which has caused death in a considerable number of cases. In several of these cases, healthy people died, and these catastrophes were clearly due to the poisonous effect of chloroform, and to that cause alone.
>
> These facts being perfectly well known to the medical world, we could not imagine that any one had taken the responsibility of suggesting the use of chloroform to her Majesty during a perfectly natural childbirth.
>
> We know that a huge amount of agony is avoided through chloroform but its *unnecessary* use should not be suggested, especially as the actions of royalty are quickly copied by many people.

Source C: From Robert Reid, *Microbes and Men*, published in 1974.

> Chance had not been a factor in Lister's discovery. He had read of Pasteur's germ theory of disease and had applied it. Millions of lives were saved by the new idea of antisepsis. Lister had shown how to defeat the frightful spectre which had haunted operating theatres.

Source D: A photograph showing an operation in the London Metropolitan Hospital in 1896.

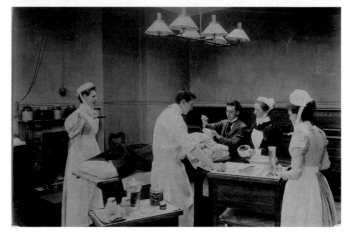

What knowledge of your own do you have about the work of Simpson and Lister?

Now plan your answer.

- Why was the development of anaesthetics a good thing in surgery?
- What did Simpson do?
- How big an effect did his work have?
- Why was the development of antiseptics a good thing in surgery?
- What did Lister do?
- How big an effect did his work have?

Finally, make sure you compare their achievements – and explain what criteria you are using to make your judgement.

- How it affected the patient
- What other surgeons thought
- Whether their work was a breakthrough or a development of an existing idea.

Mark your answers

The mark scheme is divided into levels and the first thing the examiner does is to decide what sort of answer is provided and which level to award. There are four marks available in each level and this will depend on the range of detail offered, how far the analysis is sustained throughout the essay and the quality of written English.

Notice that it is not possible to reach levels 3 and 4 without providing a reasonable amount of detail and the answer cannot score above 8 marks if the sources are not used and will not get more than 10 marks if it does not use sources and additional knowledge.

- Level 1 (1–4 marks) is for a very generalised answer or an answer that offers accurate but very limited details.
- Level 2 (5–8 marks) is awarded for an answer that has a range of accurate details but these are not used to answer the specific question; Level 2 answers often tell the story of what happened.
- Level 3 answers (9–12 marks) have recognised the focus of the question and the information is shaped into a suitable explanation.
- Level 4 (13–16 marks) is awarded for an answer that has weighed up the evidence and explained how a conclusion has been reached.

Activities

1 Read the two sample answers and decide what marks you would give them.

2 Check the examiner's comments about these two answers.

3 Now write your own answer to this question and mark yourself.

Answer A

Simpson made a very great contribution to the advances of surgery because he discoverd chloroform. He wanted to find a replacement for ether and invited some friends to join him in testing chemicals. When his wife found them all unconscious, he realised that chloroform was a good anaesthetic. Lots of people were opposed to the use of chloroform, especially in childbirth, because in the Bible God said women will have pain in childbirth so they felt this was going against God's will. Some surgeons also opposed it because they felt patients who were awake and feeling pain were less likley to die during an operation than someone who was unconscious. The use of chloroform became very popular after Queen Victoria used it for the birth of her child. She called it 'the blessed chloroform' and after than many people accepted it.
Simpson was knighted for his services to medicine.

Answer B

Lister's discovery of antiseptics can be described as an advance in surgery because it saved many lives. Infection had 'haunted operating theatres' and caused the deaths of many patients, so Lister's discovery of a way to fight infection was extremely important. Source D shows how his ideas were put into practice in hospitals. He also deserves the credit for the discovery because it was not a chance discovery – he read about Pasteur's germ theory and tried to relate it to infection in operations. This shows he was both clever and determined.

Examiner's comments

Answer A provides a lot of detail about Simpson and anaesthetics but does not explain why this was an advance in surgery and does not mention Lister at all. The details are accurate so this would be a Level 2 answer and would not lose marks even though it does not use the sources. However, since it does not mention Lister, it would not get the top mark in Level 2. The answer would receive 7 marks.

Answer B also only deals with one person – Lister. However, the answer is much more clearly focused on the effects of Lister's work and why this is an advance in surgery so this is a Level 3 answer. It will only receive the bottom mark in Level 3 because it only uses the information in the sources and there is no additional information. This answer would receive 9 marks.

Notice that the shorter answer receives the higher mark because it has understood and tried to answer the key point of the question – explaining how the work of Simpson and Lister led to advances in surgery.

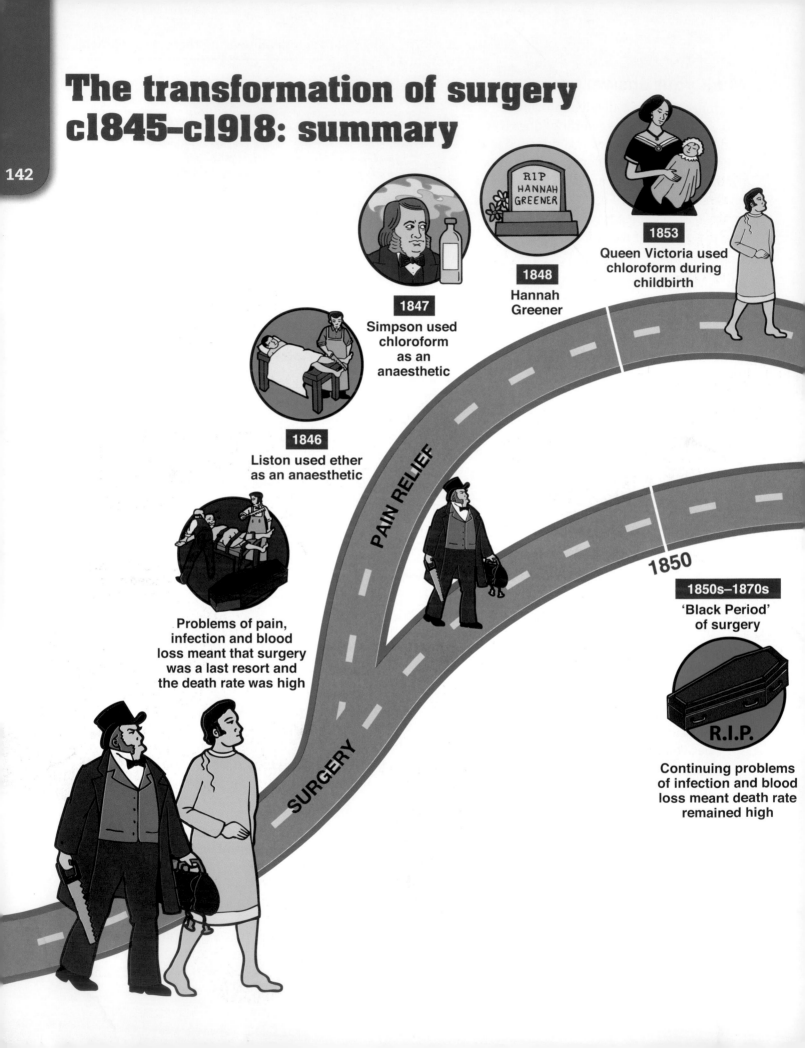

The transformation of surgery c1845–c1918: summary

142

1847 Simpson used chloroform as an anaesthetic

1848 Hannah Greener

1853 Queen Victoria used chloroform during childbirth

1846 Liston used ether as an anaesthetic

Problems of pain, infection and blood loss meant that surgery was a last resort and the death rate was high

PAIN RELIEF

SURGERY

1850

1850s–1870s 'Black Period' of surgery

R.I.P.

Continuing problems of infection and blood loss meant death rate remained high

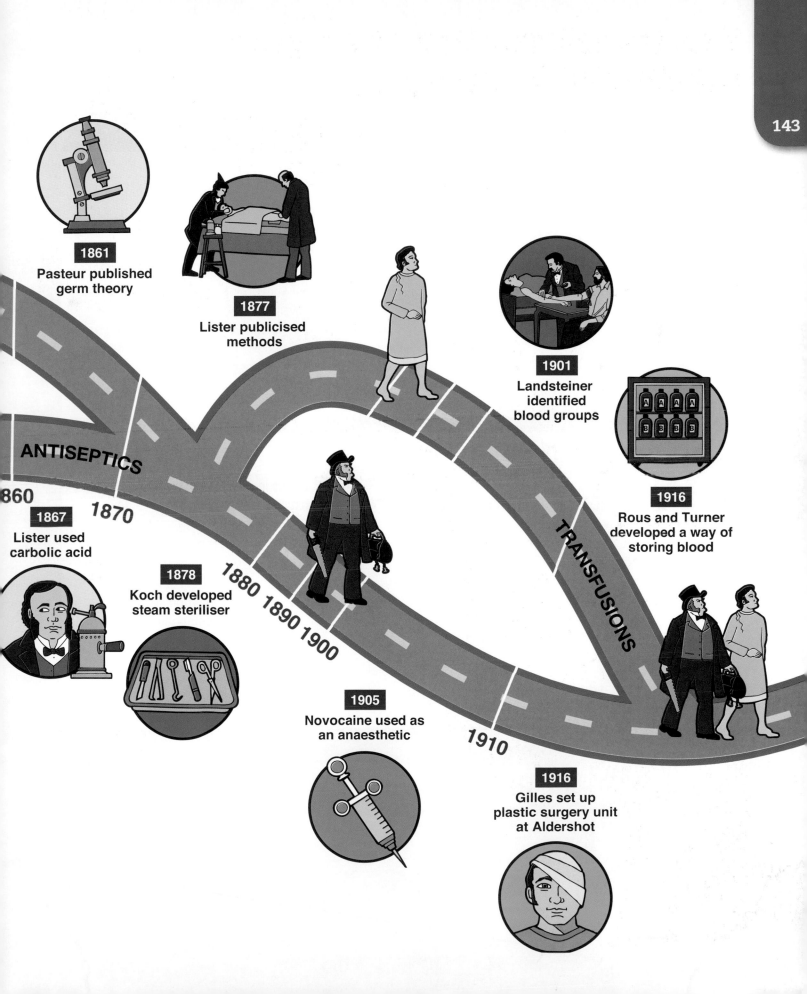

1861
Pasteur published germ theory

1877
Lister publicised methods

1901
Landsteiner identified blood groups

1916
Rous and Turner developed a way of storing blood

ANTISEPTICS

860

1867
Lister used carbolic acid

1870

1878
Koch developed steam steriliser

1880 1890 1900

TRANSFUSIONS

1905
Novocaine used as an anaesthetic

1910

1916
Gilles set up plastic surgery unit at Aldershot

Introduction

This unit tests your understanding of the way that a historian uses sources. Because it is important to understand what a source is about and to know about a source's origins and how representative it is of the situation at the time, this work has been set in the context of a period of dramatic changes in surgery. Your knowledge of this topic will help you to evaluate and use the sources, but you are not expected to have any other knowledge of medicine at this time and you will not get marks for including it in your answers.

In the exam you will have 1 hour and 15 minutes to answer five questions. You do not have any choice in

the questions in this exam so you need to make sure you have covered the whole specification and you are prepared for the sorts of question that are likely to be asked.

All the questions will focus on evidence skills, but you will need your knowledge of the topic to help you understand and evaluate the sources. However, the final question will say that you must use the sources and your own knowledge in your answer. The mark scheme has a cut off point at 10 marks out of 16 if you do not use both the sources and your own knowledge.

Checklist (factual details)

The key factual themes throughout this unit are:

- dealing with pain, for example the importance of the discovery of anaesthetics, the problems in using ether and chloroform, the work of Simpson, and changing attitudes towards anaesthetics

- dealing with infection, for example Lister's use of carbolic acid, the reactions of other doctors, and the development of antiseptic and aseptic conditions

- dealing with blood loss, for example the use of ligatures and the importance of the development of transfusions

- the role of factors in these developments, for example showing the importance of scientific knowledge and technology, communications, changing attitudes, etc.

- the extent of progress within surgery, for example weighing up the advantages of anaesthetics against the problems caused when surgeons began to do more internal operations without a proper understanding of germs and the need for antiseptics.

Support activity

You may find it helpful to do a series of ideas maps like this one:

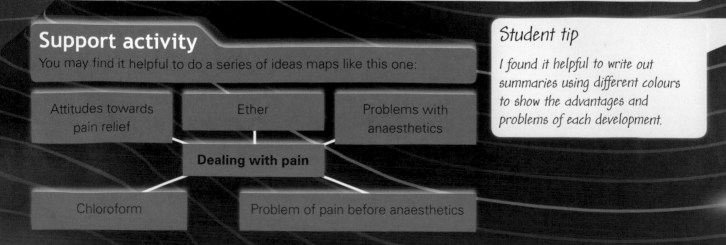

Student tip

I found it helpful to write out summaries using different colours to show the advantages and problems of each development.

Checklist (evidence skills)

The questions in this unit test five key areas:

- inference – your ability to work things out from the source, for example what you can work out about a situation, the attitude of the author, the message of a cartoon, the purpose of a speech

- analysis of the source – which parts of the source create a certain impression, which parts of a source support or challenge an idea or another source

- cross-referencing – checking how far sources agree with each other and considering the overall weight of evidence

- evaluation of reliability or usefulness – the use of various checks to see how reliable or useful a source is

- making a judgement – weighing up all the evidence on an issue in order to come to a thoughtful and supported conclusion.

ResultsPlus
Watch out!

Students often remember to give both sides of an issue but they do not weigh them up properly in order to reach a conclusion. Make it clear how you are reaching your judgement.

- Are you deciding which source is more useful to the historian by looking at which source gives you inside information from the people involved, which source tells you about the overall context, or which source gives you insight into people's attitudes?

- When you make a judgement about how important something has been, do you decide on the basis of how much it changed the situation, how quickly it became widely accepted, or how many of the problems it solved?

Support activity

Weigh up all the different elements of the source as you decide how useful it is:

Content – how helpful is it?	Source A	Source B
Content – is there added value/weakness due to details, e.g. eyewitnesses or 'loaded' language?		
Origins – any added value/weakness due to the author's involvement? Was the account written long after the event?		
Purpose – is there any added value/ weakness due to the purpose or intended audience?		
Selection – are there any signs of deliberately selecting/missing out key information? How representative is this source?		

Student tip

I found it helpful when the teacher gave us the mark scheme and I could see for myself why my answer didn't get full marks. I realised that I always need to go back and check my answers to see whether I have stayed focused on the question and whether I have backed up my comments with evidence.

Support activity

You may find it helpful to think in terms of weighing sources on scales or a seesaw.

How important was the discovery of antiseptics?

Some surgeons resisted the introduction of antiseptics at first

Side effects of carbolic acid

Blood loss still a problem

Some surgeons began to use antiseptic methods

Lister's records show reduced number of deaths after antiseptics were used

ResultsPlus
Maximise your marks

How can you tell from Source A that Simpson thought that anaesthetics were an advance in surgery? (8 marks)

Source A: From a speech by James Simpson to a meeting of doctors in Edinburgh in 1847.

In years to come people will look back with sorrow at our reactions to anaesthetics. They will be amazed at the idea of humane men saying they prefer operating on patients who are conscious instead of anaesthetised, and that the fearful agonies of an operation should be endured quietly.

Student answer

Simpson uses words that emphasise how bad surgery without anaesthetics was and suggests that in the future anaesthetics would be taken for granted.

Examiner comments

This has made the right points but the student has not backed up the comments with evidence from the source. It would also be good to explain his use of the word 'humane' to emphasise the suffering of the patient and how amazing it was that any kind of person would prefer that.

Improved student answer

Simpson uses words that emphasise how bad surgery without anaesthetics was, such as 'fearful agonies' and emphasises that in the future people would be 'amazed' and full of 'sorrow' that some doctors did not use anaesthetics and uses the word 'humane' to stress how unfair such an attitude is. He suggests that in the future anaesthetics would be taken for granted.

Study Source B. How useful is this source to the historian who is enquiring about developments in anaesthetics in the mid-19th century? (6 marks. This question in the examination would ask you to compare two sources, and the question would then be worth 10 marks.)

Source B: Snow's chloroform inhaler, invented in 1848.

Student answer

This source is useful because the inhaler wouldn't have been made if they weren't using chloroform regularly. The picture makes it look easy to use and suggests it didn't feel uncomfortable. However, it doesn't tell us how many people used these inhalers or whether there were any problems from using them and it doesn't tell us about any other anaesthetics used at this time.

Examiner comments

This answer makes good use of the content of the source to explain how it helps the historian to know that chloroform was being used. It also points out the limitations of the source and says clearly what it doesn't tell the historian. However, the answer only talks about the content of the source and therefore it is Level 2 and would receive 4 marks. To get a Level 3 mark, it must include some consideration of the nature or origins of the source. It is an illustration, not a photograph, which could mean that this had not yet been used in real life, or it could mean that it was being publicised by Snow so that more people could use it or by the people who would manufacture and sell it. Ideally, the answer would point out that we cannot tell from this source whether the inhaler was being used but it does show people were trying to find ways to improve the way anaesthetics were administered.

Improved student answer

This source is useful because the inhaler wouldn't have been made if they weren't using chloroform regularly. The very fact that there is an illustration showing the correct use of the inhaler suggests that a number of the inhalers had already been sold and were in use, or that it was an advertisement to increase the number of inhalers being used. The picture makes it look easy to use and suggests it didn't feel uncomfortable. However, it doesn't tell us how many people used these inhalers or whether there were any problems from using them and doesn't tell us about any other anaesthetics used at this time. It also tells us nothing about how or why it was developed or why the illustration was produced.

'Surgery in the 19th century improved significantly with the use of anaesthetics.' Use Sources C, D and E and your own knowledge to explain how far you agree with this statement. (16 marks)

Source C: A comment from Dr Wilkinson, the keeper of the historical documents for the Royal Society of Anaesthetists.

On 19 December 1846 in Dumfries ether was used to amputate the leg of a patient who had been run over by a cart; it is believed that the patient died. Two days later, at University College Hospital, London, Robert Liston amputated the leg of a chauffeur, Frederick Churchill, while a medical student called William Squires gave an ether anaesthetic to the patient.

It is difficult to understand today how major this advance was. Before this, surgery was a terrifying last resort in a final attempt to save life. Few operations were possible and the key to being a successful surgeon was speed. Most patients were held or strapped down – some would mercifully faint from their agony – many died, either on the table or shortly afterwards. The suffering was intense.

Source D: From Simpson's *Account of an Anaesthetic Agent* published in 1847.

From the time when I first saw ether being successfully used, I was convinced that we would find other substances which could achieve the same effects. I have talked about this with various professional friends, who know more about chemistry than I do, and I have had different drugs manufactured for me by the local chemist. The one which I have found most effective is chloroform and I have tried it on more than thirty individuals.

The advantage of using chloroform rather than ether is that less chloroform is needed to achieve the same state of unconsciousness; it works more quickly than ether; it is more agreeable to inhale and the odour does not remain on someone's breath or clothes.

Source E: An operation at the Metropolitan Hospital in 1896 showing the use of anaesthetics.

Student answer

Surgery before anaesthetics was very painful and therefore surgeons aimed to be as quick as possible. This meant that only simple operations could be done and surgeons did not dare risk doing surgery inside the chest or the stomach. The discovery of ether as an anaesthetic was a very important step in progress in surgery because the patient was not in pain and was not struggling. This meant the surgeon could take longer and do a more careful job.

The use of ether caused some problems because it tended to irritate the lungs of the patient and make them cough during the operation. It also made people vomit sometimes and was highly flammable. Therefore James Simpson searched for a better anaesthetic and discovered chloroform.

Although some people opposed the use of anaesthetics, particularly for childbirth, most people quickly accepted it, and when Queen Victoria used chloroform for the birth of her eighth child it was seen to be accepted.

However, chloroform was not completely safe and it was difficult to measure the dose, so some people died, such as Hannah Greener during an operation to remove her toenail. There were also other problems because anaesthetics encouraged surgeons to try out more complex operations and when they put their dirty hands and instruments into the open wound they were actually making infection worse. For this reason the death rate rose. Furthermore, there was still the problem of blood loss – which became more of a problem if the operations went on for too long or went deep into the body.

Although anaesthetics were a significant breakthrough and did lead to progress in surgery in the 19th century, the real improvements did not come until the problems of infection and blood loss had also been dealt with, so anaesthetics alone did not lead to significant improvements.

Examiner comments

This answer shows excellent understanding of the issue, and excellent knowledge is used to back up the comments. It shows the problems with operations before anaesthetics, the significance of the discovery of anaesthetics, problems and improvements in anaesthetics and then weighs those advances against the remaining problems of infection and blood loss. This answer deserves full marks BUT there is no mention of the sources so the maximum it could receive is 10 out of 16.

Improved student answer

Surgery before anaesthetics was very painful and therefore surgeons aimed to be as quick as possible. This meant that only simple operations could be done and surgeons did not dare risk doing surgery inside the chest or stomach. The use of anaesthetics helped to relieve pain which was a major problem in surgery in the 19th century and therefore it was a significant improvement. Surgeons now felt they could develop their skill further rather than having to act as quickly as possible and surgery seemed less like butchery. Source C stresses this when it says that 'surgery was a terrifying last resort'.

However, the use of ether caused some problems because it tended to irritate the lungs of the patient and make them cough during the operation. It also made people vomit sometimes and was highly flammable. Therefore James Simpson searched for a better anaesthetic and discovered chloroform and the benefits of chloroform are described in Source B. The fact that it was used in many hospitals is shown in Source E but some people opposed the use of anaesthetics, particularly for childbirth. Nevertheless, most people quickly accepted it and when Queen Victoria used chloroform for the birth of her eighth child it was seen to be accepted.

However, chloroform was not completely safe and it was difficult to measure the dose, so some people died. Anaesthetics encouraged surgeons to try out more complex operations and when they put their dirty hands and instruments into the open wound they were actually making infection worse. For this reason the death rate rose. Furthermore, there was still the problem of blood loss – which became more of a problem if the operations went on for too long or went deep into the body.

Although anaesthetics were a significant breakthrough and did lead to progress in surgery in the 19th century, the real improvements did not come until the problems of infection and blood loss had also been dealt with, so anaesthetics alone did not lead to significant improvements.

Welcome to examzone

Revising for your exams can be a daunting prospect. In this part of the book we'll take you through the best way of revising for your exams, step by step, to ensure you get the best results possible.

Zone In!

Have you ever become so absorbed in a task that suddenly it feels entirely natural and easy to perform? This is a feeling familiar to many athletes and performers. They work hard to recreate it in competition in order to do their very best. It's a feeling of being 'in the zone', and if you can achieve that same feeling in an examination, the chances are you'll perform brilliantly.

The good news is that you can get 'in the zone' by taking some simple steps in advance of the exam. Here are our top tips.

UNDERSTAND IT

Make sure you understand the exam process and what revision you need to do. This will give you confidence and also help you to get things into proportion. These pages are a good place to find some starting pointers for performing well in exams.

FRIENDS AND FAMILY

Make sure that your friends and family know when you want to revise. Even share your revision plan with them. Learn to control your times with them, so you don't get distracted. This means you can have better quality time with them when you aren't revising, because you aren't worrying about what you ought to be doing.

DEAL WITH DISTRACTIONS

Think about the issues in your life that may interfere with revision. Write them all down. Then think about how you can deal with each so they don't affect your revision.

COMPARTMENTALISE

You might not be able to deal with all the issues that can distract you. For example, you may be worried about a friend who is ill, or just be afraid of the exam. In this case, there is still a useful technique you can use. Put all of these worries into an imagined box in your mind at the start of your revision (or in the exam) and mentally lock it. Only open it again at the end of your revision session (or exam).

DIET AND EXERCISE

Make sure you eat sensibly and exercise as well! If your body is not in the right state, how can your mind be? A substantial breakfast will set you up for the day, and a light evening meal will keep your energy levels high.

BUILD CONFIDENCE

Use your revision time not only to revise content, but also to build your confidence in readiness for tackling the examination. For example, try tackling a short sequence of easy tasks in record time.

Planning Zone

The key to success in exams and revision often lies in good planning. Knowing **what** you need to do and **when** you need to do it is your best path to a stress-free experience. Here are some top tips in creating a great personal revision plan.

First of all, **know your strengths and weaknesses**.

Go through each topic making a list of how well you think you know the topic. Use your mock examination results and/or any other test results that are available as a check on your self-assessment. This will help you to plan your personal revision effectively, putting extra time into your weaker areas.

Next, *create your plan!*

Remember to make time for considering how topics interrelate.

For example, in History you will be expected to know not just the date when an event happened, but why it happened, how important it was, and how one event relates to another.

The specification quite clearly states when you are expected to be able to link one topic to another so plan this into your revision sessions.

You will be tested on this in the exam and you can gain valuable marks by showing your ability to do this.

Finally, *follow the plan!*

You can use the revision sections in the following pages to kick-start your revision.

MAY

SUNDAY	MONDAY	TUES
30	30	1

Be realistic about how much time you can devote to your revision, but also make sure you put in enough time. Give yourself regular breaks or different activities to give your life some variance. Revision need not be a prison sentence!

Find out your exam dates. Go to the Edexcel website to find all final exam dates, and check with your teacher.

iew Sectic
complete t
ractice ex
question

Chunk your revision in each subject down into smaller sections. This will make it more manageable and less daunting.

Draw up a list of all the dates from the start of your revision right through to your exams.

13

Review Sectio
Complete three
practice exam

20

Review Sectio
Try the Keywor
Quiz again

Make sure you allow time for assessing your progress against your initial self-assessment. Measuring progress will allow you to see and be encouraged by your improvement. These little victories will build your confidence.

22

EXAM DAY!

27

28

29

Don't Panic Zone

152

As you get close to completing your revision, the Big Day will be getting nearer and nearer. Many students find this the most stressful time and tend to go into panic mode, either working long hours without really giving their brains a chance to absorb information or giving up and staring blankly at the wall.

Panicking simply makes your brain seize up and you find that information and thoughts simply cannot flow naturally. You become distracted and anxious, and things seem worse than they are. Many students build the exams up into more than they are. Remember: the exams are not trying to catch you out! If you have studied the course, there will be no surprises on the exam paper!

Student tip

I know how silly it is to panic, especially if you've done the work and know your stuff. I was asked by a teacher to produce a report on a project I'd done, and I panicked so much I spent the whole afternoon crying and worrying. I asked other people for help, but they were panicking too. In the end, I calmed down and looked at the task again. It turned out to be quite straightforward and, in the end, I got my report finished first and it was the best of them all!

In the exam you don't have much time, so you can't waste it by panicking. The best way to control panic is simply to do what you have to do. Think carefully for a few minutes, then start writing and as you do, the panic will drain away.

ExamZone

For the **Medicine and treatment** paper, you will have an hour and a quarter for the exam, and in that time you have to answer four questions. You need to answer Questions 1 and 2. Then you must choose to answer one question from Questions 3 and 4, and then choose to answer one question from Questions 5 and 6.

For the **Transformation of surgery** paper, you will have an hour and a quarter and in that time you have to answer five questions. There are no choices for this exam.

Each question on each paper is worth a different number of marks and it is important that you use your time effectively. Don't waste precious time on a 4-mark question that might then leave you with too little time to spend on a question which is worth 16 marks!

Don't panic

Meet the exam paper

This diagram shows the front cover of the exam paper. These instructions, information and advice will always appear on the front of the paper. It is worth reading it carefully now. Check you understand it. Now is a good opportunity to ask your teacher about anything you are not sure of here.

Print your surname here, and your other names afterwards. This is an additional safeguard to ensure that the exam board awards the marks to the right candidate.

Here you fill in the school's exam number.

Ensure that you understand exactly how long the examination will last, and plan your time accordingly.

Note that the quality of your written communication will also be marked. Take particular care to present your thoughts and work at the highest standard you can, for maximum marks.

Here you fill in your personal exam number. Take care when writing it down because the number is important to the exam board when writing your score.

In this box, the examiner will write the total marks you have achieved in the exam paper.

Make sure that you understand exactly which questions from which sections you should attempt.

Don't feel that you have to fill the answer space provided. Everybody's handwriting varies, so a long answer from you may take up as much space a short answer from someone else.

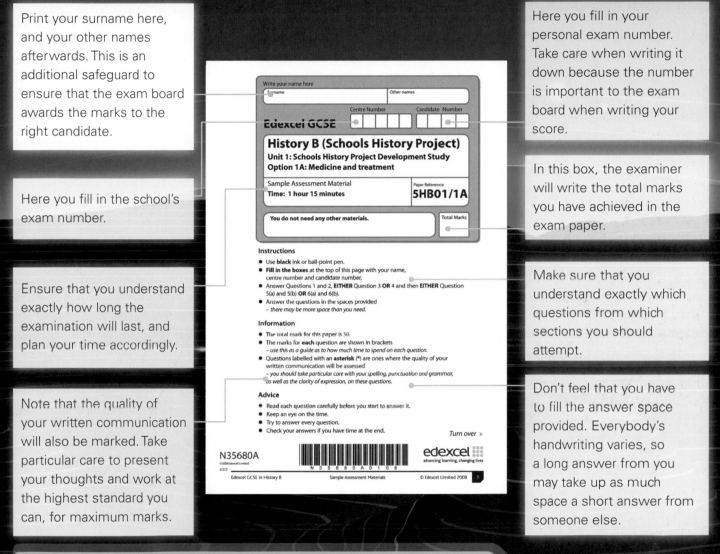

Understanding the language of the exam paper

Outline	Provide more than one point or reason. At least two or more reasons are necessary to reach Level 3.
Describe	The examiner is looking for a concise and organised account. Jot down three or four points in the margin that you want to include in your answer. Arrange them in the most logical order.
Explain how	The examiner is trying to discover whether you understand the key ideas about how and why developments happened in the history of medicine. The more detail you can give, the more marks you will receive.
Give reasons for your answer	You need to provide an explanation.
Do you agree?	You are free to agree or disagree. What makes a difference is how well you back up your case.

ZoneOut

This section provides answers to the most common questions students have about what happens after they complete their exams. For more information, visit www. heinemann.co.uk/hotlinks (express code 4400P) and click on ExamZone.

About your grades

Whether you've done better than, worse than, or just as you expected, your grades are the final measure of your performance on your course and in the exams. On this page we explain some of the information that appears on your results slip and tell you what to do if you think something is wrong. We answer the most common questions about grades and look at some of the options facing you.

When will my results be published?

Results for summer examinations are issued on the **middle** two Thursdays in August, with GCE first and GCSE second. January exam results are issued in March.

Can I get my results online?

Visit www.heinemann.co.uk/hotlinks (express code 4400P) and click on Results Plus, where you will find detailed student results information including the 'Edexcel Gradeometer' which demonstrates how close you were to the nearest grade boundary. You will need a password to access this information, which can be retrieved from your school's exam secretary.

I haven't done as well as I expected. What can I do now?

First of all, talk to your subject teacher. After all the teaching that you have had, tests and internal examinations, he/she is the person who best knows what grade you are capable of achieving. Take your results slip to your subject teacher, and go through the information on it in detail. If you both think there is something wrong with the result, the school or college can apply to see your completed examination paper and then, if necessary, ask for a re-mark immediately. The original mark can be confirmed or lowered, as well as raised, as a result of a re-mark.

How do my grades compare with those of everybody else who sat this exam?

You can compare your results with those of others in the UK who have completed the same examination using the information on Edexcel website at www.heinemann.co.uk/hotlinks (express code 4400P) by clicking on Edexcel.

I achieved a higher mark for the same unit last time. Can I use that result?

Yes. The higher score is the one that goes towards your overall grade. The best result will be used automatically when the overall grade is calculated. You do not need to ask the exam board to take into account a previous result. This will be done automatically so you can be assured that all your best unit results have gone into calculating your overall grade.

What happens if I was ill over the period of my examinations?

If you become ill before or during the examination period you are eligible for special consideration. This also applies if you have been affected by an accident, bereavement or serious disturbance during an examination.

If my school has requested special consideration for me, is this shown on my Statement of Results?

If your school has requested special consideration for you, it is not shown on your results slip, but it will be shown on a subject mark report that is sent to your school or college. If you want to know whether special consideration was requested for you, you should ask your Examinations Officer.

Can I have a re-mark of my examination paper?

Yes, this is possible, but remember that only your school or college can apply for a re-mark, not you or your parents/carers. First of all, you should consider carefully whether or not to ask your school or college to make a request for a re-mark. It is worth knowing that very few re-marks result in a change to a grade – not because Edexcel is embarrassed that a change of marks has been made, but simply because a re-mark request has shown that the original marking was accurate. Check the closing date for re-marking requests with your Examinations Officer.

When I asked for a re-mark of my paper, my subject grade went down. What can I do?

There is no guarantee that your grades will go up if your papers are re-marked. They can also go down or stay the same. After a re-mark, the only way to improve your grade is to take the examination again. Your school or college Examinations Officer can tell you when you can do that.

How many times can I re-sit a unit?

You may re-sit a modular GCSE Science or Mathematics module test once, prior to taking your terminal examination and before obtaining your final overall grade. The highest score obtained on either the first attempt or the re-sit counts towards your final grade. If you enter a module in GCSE Mathematics at a different tier, this does not count as a re-sit. If you are on the modular History GCSE course, and sat the first unit last year, you may re-sit module 1 when you sit module 2 to maximise your full course grade.

For much more information, go to www.heinemann.co.uk/hotlinks (express code 4400P) and click on ExamZone.

Glossary

This Glossary contains all the key word definitions, plus some other terms used in the book that may be unfamiliar to you. When appropriate the definitions are particularly directed to the period being studied.

Ague – An old term for illnesses that involve fever and fits of shivering.

Almshouse – A house founded by charity, offering accommodation for the poor.

Alternative medicine – Medicine that uses herbs and other natural remedies, as well as therapies such as acupuncture, instead of drugs.

Amputation – The cutting off of a limb – for example, an arm or a leg – from the body.

Anaesthetic – A substance that affects your nervous system so that you are less aware of sensation and don't feel pain.

Anatomy – The structure of the body, for example bones, nerves, muscles.

Antibiotics – Drugs that stop infections caused by **bacteria**.

Antibodies – Special cells created by the body to fight infection and disease.

Antiseptic – Something that fights against **sepsis** and the **microbes** that create infection.

Apothecary – A person who made medicines and ointments using ingredients such as herbs and spices.

Appendix – A tube-shaped sac attached to the large intestine; appendicitis occurs when it is inflamed.

Artery – A blood vessel that carries blood from the heart to all parts of the body.

Aseptic – Sterile; free from the **microbes** that cause infection.

Astrology – The study of the stars and planets and how they are thought to affect humans and nature.

Asylum – An old type of hospital for those who were mentally ill.

Bacteria – Micro-organisms that live in soil, water, plants and animals and that can cause diseases.

Bile – A thick, bitter fluid produced by the liver; a liquid once thought to be one of the **Four Humours**.

Black Death – A highly infectious disease that spread throughout Europe in the mid-14th century.

Bloodletting – The drawing of blood from a patient by a doctor.

Body snatcher – A person who used to obtain dead bodies illegally and sell them to medical schools for dissection.

By-law – A law made by a town's local authority that affects only that town.

Cautery – The use of heat to seal blood vessels and stop bleeding.

Cesspit – A pit for the disposal of liquid waste and sewage, for homes that aren't connected to a **sewer**.

Chamber pot – A 'potty' that was kept in a room or chamber, for people who needed the toilet and did not go to the outside privy or **latrine**.

Chromosomes – Thread-like structures found in most living cells that carry **genetic** information.

Church, The – The international organisation of all Christian believers.

Cloning – Using cells from one organism to make another identical organism.

Consultant – A doctor specialising in a specific disease or part of the body; usually based in hospital and seeing patients referred by a **general practitioner (GP)**.

Crystallography – Using radiation to take a high-power X-ray photograph.

Curare – A poison obtained from South American plants and used as an **anaesthetic**.

Diagnosis – Identifying an illness by examining the symptoms.

Dialysis – Removal of impurities from the blood by a kidney machine.

Dissection – Cutting open a body to examine its internal structure.

DNA – The abbreviation for deoxyribonucleic acid, which contains the genetic instructions for every cell in your body.

Druid – A priest or magician of the ancient Celtic religion.

Endoscope – An instrument with a tiny camera on the end that can be used to look at the internal parts of the body.

Epidemic – A severe outbreak of an infectious disease.

Ethics – A set of moral principles followed by members of a profession, such as medical ethics.

Flagellants – People who whip themselves as a punishment and to show God that they are sorry.

Folk remedies – Traditional remedies practised by ordinary people, not doctors, and passed down through history, often by word of mouth.

Four Humours – A theory that developed in Ancient Greece to explain illness.

Gall bladder – The sac attached to the liver that stores **bile**.

Gangrene – Occurs when body tissue dies, which can be caused by infection or bad circulation.

General practitioner (GP) – A doctor who works in a practice dealing directly with the public.

Genetics – The study of genes and inherited characteristics.

Herbals – Books containing descriptions of plants used in herbal medicine.

Hereditary – Passed on from one generation of a family to another.

Hygiene – Conditions or practices, especially cleanliness, that maintain health and prevent disease.

Hypnotism – Putting a person into a trance-like state that is like sleep, but in which the person readily accepts suggestions and acts on them.

Immunisation – Making immune to infection, usually by **vaccination**.

Industrial – Connected to industry and manufacturing.

Industrial revolution – The period c1750–c1900 when there were rapid changes in the way work and industry were organised.

Inoculation – A way of giving a patient a mild dose of an illness so that the body builds up its immunity.

Journal – (1) An account that is written up at regular intervals, like a diary – this is a personal and private source. (2) A published set of articles (like an academic magazine), for example *The Lancet* is a respected medical journal containing articles by doctors and researchers.

Laissez-faire – The idea that government should not interfere too much with industry and private business.

Latrine – A toilet, especially a communal one, often in an army camp, for example.

Leech – A blood-sucking worm used to draw blood from a patient; also an old name for a **physician**.

Ligature – A thread tied around a blood vessel to stop bleeding.

Magic bullet – A chemical drug that kills the **microbes** causing a specific disease without harming the rest of the body.

Malaria – 'Bad air'; people used to believe that malaria was a fever caused by poisonous air arising from marshes. The illness is now known to be caused by mosquitoes.

Medieval – A name for the 'Middle Ages', the period between the Ancient World (which ended when the Romans left Britain) and the Renaissance of the 16th and 17th centuries.

Miasma – The theory that disease is caused by poisonous vapours in the air.

Microbes – Micro-organisms, especially **bacteria** causing disease.

Midwife – A woman, or nowadays also a man, who assists women in childbirth.

National Health Service (NHS) – An organisation set up by the government in 1948 to give free health care to all.

Obesity – The state of being grossly fat or overweight.

Opium – An addictive drug prepared from the juice of the poppy, which can be used to ease pain.

Patent medicine – A mixture that has been created by one person or company and is sold under a particular brand name.

Pharmaceutical industry – The business of manufacturing medicinal drugs, prescribed by a doctor or sold by a chemist.

Pharmacy – A business selling medical drugs; a chemist's.

Physician – A trained doctor.

Physiology – The way organs function within the body, for example the work of the heart, liver and kidneys.

Plastic surgery – Surgery carried out in order to change the appearance of the patient.

Prescription charges – Payment for medicine that has been prescribed by a doctor.

Prosthetic limb – Artificial arm or leg, often made from metal and plastic.

Public health – The standard of living conditions and general health of the people.

Public health provision – Health provision for the whole community, such as the provision of fresh water, **sewers** and the availability of health care.

Purging – Getting rid of bad or excess humours by making someone sick or by making them have diarrhoea.

Quarantine – The situation where someone who may have an infectious disease is isolated from other people to try to prevent the disease spreading; often the whole family is isolated.

Radiotherapy – The use of radiation in medicine, often to attack cancer.

Reformation – A period of challenges and divisions within the Christian Church.

Renaissance – A period in the 16th and 17th centuries when people thought they were reviving Ancient Greek and Ancient Roman culture but also made new discoveries.

Royal Society – A group set up in 1660 to enable educated people to discuss scientific ideas.

Sanitation – Measures for the promotion of health and prevention of disease, especially the provision of drainage and **sewers**.

Sepsis – A condition in which harmful **bacteria** affect the flesh, normally leading to infection and decaying flesh.

Sewer – An underground system for removing liquid waste (sewage).

Society – The way a group of people links together in some common ways.

Spontaneous generation – The idea that rubbish or decaying material creates **microbes**.

Superbugs – **Bacteria** that have become resistant to **antibiotics**.

Supernatural – Forces outside normal nature that some people believe can affect events, for example God, charms and luck, witchcraft or **astrology**.

Surgeon – Someone who deals with wounds or with treatment that involves cutting the body.

Tourniquet – Something that is tied around a part of the body to put pressure on a blood vessel and stop the loss of blood.

Transfusion – The process of giving blood from a donor to the patient.

Vaccination – A safe way of stimulating the body's immune system against a particular disease.

Vein – A blood vessel that carries blood from all parts of the body towards the heart.

Welfare State – The coordination and provision by the government of all matters affecting the health of the people.

Workhouse – An institution where people could go if they could not support themselves; they would be expected to work in return for their food and bed.

Index

In the following index, main entries of key words are given in bold type and the page number that is also in bold will lead you to a definition of the word. For all these definitions, as well as further definitions of unfamiliar words, see the Glossary on pages 156–157.

Index